T0002075

Best Easy Day Hikes
Big Bend National Park

Help Us Keep This Guide Up to Date

Every effort has been made by the author and editors to make this guide as accurate and useful as possible. However, many things can change after a guide is published—regulations change, facilities come under new management, and so forth.

We would love to hear from you concerning your experiences with this guide and how you feel it could be improved and kept up to date. While we may not be able to respond to all comments and suggestions, we'll take them to heart, and we'll also make certain to share them with the author. Please send your comments and suggestions to falconeditorial@rowman.com.

Thanks for your input!

Best Easy Day Hikes Series

Best Easy Day Hikes Big Bend National Park

Laurence Parent

FALCONGUIDES

ESSEX, CONNECTICUT

FALCONGUIDES®

An imprint of Globe Pequot, the trade division of
The Rowman & Littlefield Publishing Group, Inc.
4501 Forbes Blvd., Ste. 200
Lanham, MD 20706
www.rowman.com

Falcon and FalconGuides are registered trademarks and Make
Adventure Your Story is a trademark of The Rowman & Littlefield
Publishing Group, Inc.

Distributed by NATIONAL BOOK NETWORK

Copyright © 2024 The Rowman & Littlefield Publishing Group, Inc.

Maps by The Rowman & Littlefield Publishing Group, Inc.

British Library Cataloguing-in-Publication Information Available

Library of Congress Cataloging-in-Publication Data Available

ISBN 978-1-4930-7824-0 (paperback: alk. paper)
ISBN 978-1-4930-7825-7 (ebook)

♾™ The paper used in this publication meets the minimum
requirements of American National Standard for Information
Sciences—Permanence of Paper for Printed Library Materials, ANSI/
NISO Z39.48-1992.

Contents

Acknowledgments.. vii
Introduction 1
How to Use This Guide... 21
Map Legend.. 27

The Hikes

 1 Santa Elena Canyon.. 28
 2 The Chimneys 32
 3 Lower Burro Mesa Pour-off 35
 4 Upper Burro Mesa 39
 5 Sam Nail Ranch.. 42
 6 Grapevine Hills... 46
 7 Window View.. 51
 8 Window 54
 9 Lost Mine 59
10 Pine Canyon... 63
11 Ernst Tinaja 65
12 Hot Springs 70
13 Rio Grande Village Nature Trail 74
14 Boquillas Canyon.. 78
15 Dog Canyon.. 82

Suggested Reading... 88
About the Author... 89

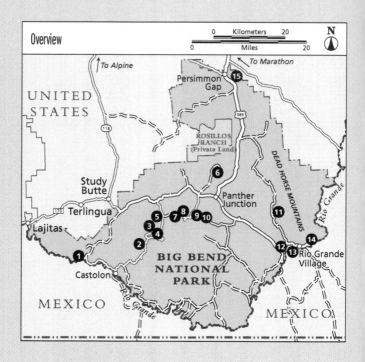

Acknowledgments

This book project was completed with the contributions of many people. Special thanks go to Tom VandenBerg, chief of interpretation at Big Bend National Park, for reviewing this book for changes and errors. Thanks also go to the members of the Big Bend National Park staff who hiked many of the park trails and wrote the first draft of some of the descriptions for my comprehensive *Hiking Big Bend* book, some of which are adapted and reused here. These hikers and writers were Audrey Ashcraft, Karen Boucher, Don Corrick, Mark Flippo, John Forsythe, Mark Herberger, Mary K. Manning, Gus Sánchez, Jeff Selleck, Raymond Skiles, and Carol Sperling.

Thanks go to David Legere and Lynn Zelem of Falcon-Guides for encouraging this project. I also wish to thank Patricia Parent, Earl Nottingham, William Hennessy, Barry Hanlon, Mary Baxter, John Morlock, Heather Ainsworth-Dobbins, David Mettauer, Michael Gentry, Steve Kennedy, and Erica Little for accompanying me on many of the hikes I did for this book. Joanna Ruley-Garza helped with the administrative work that goes with running a photography and writing business.

Introduction

To create *Best Easy Day Hikes: Big Bend National Park*, I've selected the easier, more scenic hikes from my comprehensive *Hiking Big Bend* book, also published by FalconGuides, and edited them for this new book. This book is aimed at park visitors with limited time or ability to hike the park's longer, harder trails. It is also directed at families with young children for whom the park's harder trails would be very difficult. The selected hikes are easy routes to some of the park's most scenic destinations. Trailheads are easy to find and mostly on paved roads. The selected trails are popular, well marked, and with few route-finding difficulties. The longest is 5.6 miles round-trip; most are considerably less. With the exception of the Lost Mine and Window Trails, elevation gain is generally quite modest.

For hikers and backpackers in Texas, Big Bend National Park is the state's number-one destination. More than 1,200 square miles of undeveloped land beckon with endless miles of trails and cross-country routes. The park is not only the largest tract of public land in Texas but also one of the best examples of Chihuahuan Desert in the country.

The Chihuahuan Desert sprawls across a vast expanse of northern Mexico, West Texas, and southern New Mexico. Like other deserts, it is defined as an area of low precipitation, generally less than 10 inches per year at lower elevations. Specific plant communities and climate patterns differentiate the Chihuahuan Desert from other deserts. One plant in particular, the lechuguilla, is unique to the Chihuahuan Desert. The plant, growing in a green rosette of thick, fibrous leaves tipped with wicked spines, quickly makes itself apparent to unwary hikers at Big Bend.

Like islands in a sea, rugged mountain ranges dot the vast lowland expanses of the Chihuahuan Desert. Some of these mountains, such as the Chisos Mountains at Big Bend, reach high enough elevations to attract additional rainfall. The additional rain and cooler temperatures allow forests to grow on the upper slopes of these ranges. A forest of pinyon pine, juniper, and oak cloaks the Chisos Mountains; bigger ranges, such as the Sierra del Carmen across the river from the park in Mexico, contain lush forests of Arizona pine, Douglas fir, aspen, and other trees.

Water is of paramount importance in the desert country of Big Bend National Park. Plants adapt to the hot, dry terrain by growing small leaves. Waxy coatings limit transpiration of water by plants. Cacti have done away with leaves altogether. Plants such as the ocotillo only produce leaves after sufficient rainfall. Seeds of many annuals will not even germinate in dry years; when they do germinate, they develop, flower, and fruit quickly before the moisture disappears. Animals also adapt to the arid conditions. Most come out to feed and hunt only at night during cooler temperatures. The kangaroo rat never has to drink at all; it obtains water from its food.

Because water is scarce at Big Bend, springs and water holes are particularly valuable. Permanent creeks are rare. One major exception, the Rio Grande, creates a long, narrow oasis—a ribbon of green along the southern boundary of the park. The river and springs are vital to the park's wildlife.

The many trails at Big Bend National Park visit some of these springs and the deep canyons of the Rio Grande. They wander through the high, wooded peaks of the Chisos Mountains and past the ruins of old ranches and settlements. This guide will lead you to many places that park visitors unwilling to leave their cars will never see. Some of the most spectacular scenery in Texas awaits you.

Backcountry Ethics—Leave No Trace

A few simple rules and courtesies will help preserve the natural environment and allow others to enjoy their outdoor experiences. Every hiker has at least a slight impact on the land and other visitors. Your goal should be to minimize that impact. Some of the rules and suggestions may seem overly restrictive and confining; however, with increasing use of the parks, such rules have become more necessary. All can be followed with little inconvenience and will contribute to a better outdoor experience for you and others.

Camping

Three developed campgrounds lie within the national park—at the Chisos Basin, Rio Grande Village, and Castolon. Showers and limited RV sites with hookups can be found at Rio Grande Village. Many primitive car campsites are found along the park's back roads. Hikers have innumerable options for backcountry camping. Within the popular Chisos Mountains, backpackers must use designated sites scattered throughout the high country. A permit must be obtained online at recreation.gov or in person at Panther Junction or the Chisos Basin Visitor Center ahead of time. During busy times of year, November through April—and especially Thanksgiving, Christmas, Easter, and college spring break—it may be difficult to obtain a campsite anywhere in the park. Reserve online well ahead of time if you plan to visit then. If your plans change, be sure to cancel your reservations. Although there is often little or no refund for cancellations, it will free up the site for another park visitor. Within certain guidelines, most of the rest of the park is open to backcountry camping. As with the Chisos Mountains, you must obtain a permit, but you are not restricted to specific sites.

Camp at least 100 yards away from water sources. The vegetation at creeks and springs is often the most fragile. Camping well away prevents trampling and destruction of plant life. Destruction of vegetation usually leads to erosion and muddying of water sources. Additionally, camping 100 yards away prevents runoff of wash water, food scraps, and human waste into the water supply. In desert areas, a spring may be the only water source for miles. If you camp too close, you may keep wildlife from reaching vital water. Dry camps have advantages—they are usually warmer and attract fewer insects.

Pick a level site that won't require modification to be usable. Don't destroy vegetation as you set up camp. The ideal camp is probably on bare desert ground in the lower areas of the park. Don't trench around the tent site; choose a site with good natural drainage. If possible, pick a site that has already been used so you won't trample another. If you remove rocks, sticks, or other debris, replace them when you depart. You want to leave no trace of your visit when you go.

Be courteous—don't pitch your tent right next to other people's camp. Remember, they are probably out in the backcountry to get away from crowds, too. For similar reasons, avoid creating excessive noise. Your camp must be set up at least 100 yards away from the trail and, ideally, out of sight.

Carry out all your trash. Food containers are much lighter once the contents have been consumed and are easy to carry. Improve the area for future visitors by taking out trash others have left behind.

When available, such as in the high Chisos Mountains, use backcountry toilets. Otherwise, dig a 6- to 8-inch-deep hole as far away from water, campsites, and trails as possible and bury human wastes. Carry out toilet paper in a zip-top plastic bag along with the rest of your trash.

Because wood is scarce in desert country, fires are prohibited. In addition, wildfires can start easily in the dry terrain, and campfires leave scars that are slow to heal. For cooking purposes, backpacking stoves are much easier, quicker, and more efficient.

A few areas are closed to backcountry camping, including any sites within 0.5 mile of a road, a developed area, the Mariscal Mine, or Hot Springs. Also, don't camp within 100 yards of a historical or an archaeological site. Common sense dictates that you don't camp near a cliff edge or in a dry, flood-prone wash. Within the Chisos Mountains, several areas are closed to campers: the Basin and the north section of the Chisos Mountains, including the area along the Lost Mine Trail, Pine Canyon, Green Gulch, and the high ridge that includes Pulliam and Vernon Bailey Peaks. Two other restricted areas include the part of Burro Mesa that lies above 3,400 feet in elevation and within 100 yards of any tinaja on Mesa de Anguila.

The Trail

Don't shortcut switchbacks on the trail. Switchbacks were built to ease the grade on climbs and to limit erosion. Shortcutting, although it may be shorter, usually takes more effort and causes erosion.

Always give horses and other pack animals the right-of-way. Stand well away from the trail, and make no sudden movements or noises that could spook the animals. Motorized and mechanized vehicles, including mountain bikes, are prohibited on the national park trails described in this guide. However, mountain bikes are allowed along the many miles of back roads in the park.

Dogs are not allowed on any of the national park trails because of their potential to disturb or threaten wildlife and create sanitation problems. There are no kennels in the park, so it's best to leave your dog at home if you plan to hike. If you choose to bring your dog, be sure to pick up and dispose of your pet's poop in park trash cans.

In large part because of wildfire risks, smoking is not allowed in the park on or off trail. Exceptions are paved parking lots and adjoining sidewalks, developed campgrounds, designated backcountry campsites without vegetation, and park roads. Don't do anything to disturb the natural environment. No hunting is allowed in the park. Don't cut trees or other plants. Resist the temptation to pick wildflowers. Don't blaze trees, carve initials on rocks, or add improvements to campsites. Don't remove any American Indian relics or historic items. All such artifacts are protected by law in the parks and are important to future visitors.

Rules and regulations can be tedious, but they will help ensure that Big Bend National Park remains the gem it is for future generations.

Safety
With preparation and good judgment, few mishaps should occur on your hikes. The following sections elaborate on some of the potential hazards you may encounter on the trail. Don't let the list scare you; most mishaps are easily prevented.

Weather
More emergencies at Big Bend are probably related to weather than any other factor. Not surprisingly, heat causes

many problems in the region, particularly from April to October. The desert heat can be brutal in summer. Shade temperatures of greater than 110°F are not uncommon.

On your hikes, carry and drink adequate water. For long hikes in hot weather, plan to carry at least 1 gallon of water per person per day. Wear a broad-brimmed hat and use sunscreen. Even summer hikes in the higher altitudes of the Chisos Mountains will usually be quite warm, especially in May and June before the summer rains begin. If you do summer hikes in desert areas of the park, try to start early in the morning to avoid the worst of the heat. Don't push as hard, take frequent breaks, and carry lots of water. All but the shortest desert trails are best left for cooler times of the year.

Excessive heat and dehydration can cause many serious physical problems, from headaches and nausea to heart and kidney failure. A common effect is heat exhaustion. Symptoms of heat exhaustion include skin that is still moist and sweaty, but you may feel weak, dizzy, irritable, or nauseated or have muscle cramps. Find a cool, shady place to rest, drink plenty of liquids, and eat a few crackers or another source of salt. After you feel better, keep drinking plenty of liquids and limit physical activity. Hike out during a cooler time of day. The condition is not usually serious, but get to a doctor as soon as possible to be checked out.

Heat stroke is less common but can develop with prolonged exposure to very hot conditions. It occurs when the body's temperature regulation system stops functioning, resulting in a rapid rise in body temperature. The skin is hot, flushed, and bone-dry. Confusion and unconsciousness can quickly follow. Heat stroke is life-threatening. Immediately get the victim into the coolest available place. Remove excess clothing, and dampen skin and remaining clothing with water. Fan the victim for additional cooling. If a cool stream or pond is nearby, consider immersing the victim. You must get the body temperature down quickly. Seek medical help immediately.

At the other temperature extreme, cold can also be a hazard at Big Bend. Even in the hot desert areas, sudden thunderstorms in late summer can drench you and, at the least, make you uncomfortably cool. In the Chisos Mountains, temperatures can plummet in storms. When combined with wet clothing or lack of shelter, such conditions can lead to hypothermia.

Hypothermia occurs when the body's internal temperature falls. If conditions turn wet and cold and a member of your party begins to slur speech, shivers constantly, or becomes clumsy, sleepy, or unreasonable, immediately get the hiker into shelter and out of wet clothing. Give the victim warm liquids to drink, and get him or her into a sleeping bag with one or more people. Skin-to-skin contact conducts body heat to the victim most effectively.

The weather at Big Bend is usually very temperate in winter, but fronts and storms can blow in quickly. Snow usually blankets the mountains at least a time or two every winter. During and after such storms, park temperatures can often fall well below freezing.

It's easy to prepare for most cold-weather problems. Always take extra warm clothing, especially in winter, in the Chisos Mountains and on extended hikes. Wool and some synthetics still retain some insulating capability when wet; cotton is worthless. Rain gear is essential, especially on hikes in the mountains in late summer and early fall. Carry a reliable tent on longer trips. Hole up and wait for the bad weather to pass rather than attempting a long hike out.

Most storms at Big Bend, especially in summer, are of short duration.

Temperature extremes are not the only weather-related hazard; lightning from storms poses another threat. When thunderstorms appear, seek lower ground. Stay off hilltops and away from lone trees and open areas. Lightning makes exposed mountain peaks and ridges especially hazardous. The most common thunderstorms at Big Bend develop in mid- and late summer afternoons. Plan to start your hikes early to reach the high peaks and ridges of the Chisos Mountains by lunchtime so you can leave those areas before storms appear. If you get caught in a lightning storm, seek shelter in a low-lying grove of small, equal size trees, if possible. Put down your metal-framed packs, tripods, and metal tent poles, and move well away from them.

Although floods would not seem to be a threat in the desert terrain of Big Bend National Park, sudden downpours, especially in late summer, can turn a dry wash into a raging, muddy torrent in minutes. Stay out of narrow canyons boxed in by cliffs during heavy rains. Even though you may be in sunshine, watch the weather upstream from you. Camp well above and away from the Rio Grande. For evidence of the river's past floods, consider that mud has completely buried the Santa Elena Canyon parking area in the recent past. The river is not even in sight, yet it has risen enough to flood the parking lot. In addition, never camp in that tempting sandy site in the bottom of a dry desert wash. Storms upstream from you can send water sweeping down desert washes with unbelievable fury.

Conditioning

Good physical conditioning will make your trip safer and much more pleasant. Do not push yourself too hard, especially on the steep, higher elevation trails of the Chisos Mountains. If you have been sedentary for a long time, consider getting a physical exam before you start hiking. Ease into hiking; start with the easy hikes and graduate to more difficult ones. This guide covers mostly easy trails, but two, the Lost Mine and Window Trails, are relatively strenuous. Pick a trail that fits your ability. Do not push your party any harder or faster than its weakest member can handle comfortably. Know your limits. When you get tired, rest or turn back. Remember, you are out here to have fun.

Be prepared for the hike. Read this guidebook and the specific hike description. Study maps and other books on the area. Carry all necessary equipment to ensure your comfort and safety. Every effort has been made to create a guidebook that is as accurate and current as possible, but a few errors may still creep in. Additionally, roads and trails change. Signs can disappear, springs can dry up, roads can wash out, and trails can be rerouted. Talk to park rangers about current road and trail conditions and water sources. Check the weather forecast. Find out the abilities and desires of your hiking companions before hitting the trail.

Altitude

Only the Chisos Mountains attain a very high elevation in the park. Since the highest peak reaches only 7,825 feet, most people will have few altitude-related breathing problems on any of the hikes in this park. At most, people coming from low elevations may have a little trouble in the higher reaches of the Chisos Mountains. Until you acclimate, you may suffer from a little shortness of breath and tire more easily. A very few hikers may develop headaches, nausea, fatigue, or other mild symptoms such as swelling of the face, hands, ankles, or other body areas at the highest altitudes. Mild symptoms should not change your plans. Rest for a day or two to acclimate. Retreating 1,000 feet or so will often clear up any symptoms. Spending several days at moderate altitude before climbing high will often prevent any problems.

The Chisos Mountains are not high enough to cause the serious symptoms of altitude sickness, such as pulmonary edema (fluid collecting in the lungs) or cerebral edema (fluid accumulating in the brain), except in very rare cases. Should these symptoms develop, immediately get the victim to lower elevations and medical attention.

Companions

Pick your hiking companions wisely. Consider their experience and physical and mental fitness. Try to form groups of relatively similar physical ability. Pick a leader, especially on long trips or with large groups. Ideally, have at least one experienced hiker with the group.

Too large a group is unwieldy and diminishes the wilderness experience for yourself and others. The park limits group size to fifteen people, but an ideal size is probably four. In case of injury, one can stay with the victim, while the other two can hike out for help. Thus no one is left alone. In addition, most of the backcountry campsites in the Chisos Mountains will not accommodate more than six people.

Leave your travel plans with friends so they can send help if you do not return as planned. Ask your friends to allow some time before help is sent; trips often run later than expected.

Ideally, you should never hike alone, especially cross-country or on the park's lightly traveled trails. That said, if you do hike alone, inform family or friends of your specific travel plans. Because of the large number of hikers at Big Bend, the park staff cannot keep track of the whereabouts of every hiker. Once you set up your hiking itinerary, do not deviate from it. Otherwise, rescuers will be unable to find you should the need arise. Never forget to check in with your friends and family at the end of your hike. Nothing will aggravate rescuers more than to find that you were at a bar in Terlingua relaxing with a beer while they were stumbling around in the rain and dark looking for you.

On short busy hikes or nature trails, such as those at Santa Elena Canyon or Hot Springs, where plenty of other people are around should a mishap occur, such precautions may not be necessary.

Water

Because of the heat and dry air at Big Bend, you must drink plenty of water. In summer, at least 1 gallon per day is necessary on long hikes. Since many of the springs at Big Bend are unreliable and dependent on recent rainfall, plan to carry all the water you will need. Recent droughts have made springs even more unreliable. On some of the longer desert hikes, it can be physically difficult to carry enough water. Springs can help supplement the supply, but be sure to check ahead of time to learn the springs' current status. Regardless of their believed status, try not to arrive at a spring without at least some water. If the spring had just gone dry, you could be in a difficult situation without some reserve water.

Because water sources may be contaminated, any water used should be purified before use. You may not get sick if unpurified water is obtained directly from the head of a spring in a little-used area. However, it is best to play it safe and always treat your water.

Boiling vigorously for 1 minute in the desert areas of the park and 3 minutes in the higher elevations of the park mountains is a reliable method, but slow and fuel consuming.

Mechanical filtration units are available at most outdoors shops. Filters with very small pores strain out bacteria, viruses, cysts, and other microorganisms. Their ability to filter out the smallest organisms, such as viruses, varies from model to model. For very contaminated water, filtration should probably be used in conjunction with chemical treatment.

Chemical treatment is probably the easiest method, but it may not be as effective as filtering. Chlorination is the method used by many municipal water systems, but the use of purification tablets is probably more controllable and reliable for backpackers. They can be purchased at any outdoors store. Follow the directions carefully. Cold or cloudy water requires using more chemicals or longer treatment times. The cleaner your water is from the start, the better.

Portable ultraviolet treatment systems, such as the SteriPEN, are lightweight and effective, provided the water source is relatively clear.

Get your water from springs or upstream from trails and camps if possible. Water taken from tinajas and particularly the Rio Grande is of dubious quality. Except in an emergency, it is best to avoid Rio Grande water altogether. For day hikes, it is usually easier just to carry sufficient water for the day.

The park allows hikers doing long hikes to cache water along the route ahead of time. Unless there is a bear-proof storage unit, such as that found near the start of the Homer Wilson Ranch / Dodson Trail, be sure to store the water in bear-proof canisters. If you do cache water for a hike, write your name and expected removal date on the container. Do not leave water caches in historic buildings or other popular visitor areas. As with the water, leave food only if it is stored in a commercial bear-proof canister.

Hikers can get water before hiking at outdoor spigots at the Panther Junction Visitor Center, Rio Grande Village, and other developed areas. To conserve water in this desert country, please don't take more than 5 gallons per day.

Stream Crossings

Crossing all but the smallest of streams poses several hazards. In the desert country at Big Bend, streams are rare and small and generally pose little difficulty in crossing. Except during a flash flood, few of the drainages along the trails in this guide carry any water at all. If any do flood, however, do not attempt to cross them. Just wait; such floods subside very quickly, usually within a few hours at most. When crossing one of the few creeks that often carry water, such as Terlingua or Tornillo Creek, try to find a broad, slow-moving stretch for your ford. Be careful hopping from rock to rock; rocks are often unstable and slippery and can cause a fall or twisted ankle. Undo the waist strap on your backpack for quick removal if necessary. If the water is deep or swift-moving, use a stout walking stick for stability, or even a rope.

The Rio Grande is the one significant waterway in the park. Because of its strong currents, deep holes, invisible bottom, and poor water quality, do not swim in or try to cross the river.

Insects

One of the pleasures of hiking at Big Bend is its paucity of nuisance insects. Mosquitoes usually are no problem at all. However, they will hatch after heavy rains, even in desert regions of the parks. The most likely time is late summer. A repellent containing DEET will discourage mosquitoes and gnats from bothering you. Camp well away from the river, water holes, streams, and other wet areas. Good mosquito netting on your tent will allow a pleasant night's sleep.

A tent will also keep out nocturnal creatures such as scorpions and centipedes. Bites and stings from scorpions and centipedes found at Big Bend are painful but not usually serious. As long as you use a tent and refrain from turning over rocks or logs, you are unlikely to see any.

Unlike in much of Central and East Texas, ticks are extremely rare at Big Bend. However, they can carry serious diseases, such as Rocky Mountain spotted fever and Lyme disease, so be aware of them. Use insect repellent and at least casually check yourself every night, especially if you have been moving through brush or tall grass. If a tick attaches, remove it promptly and either kill it or remove it from areas with people or pets. Use tweezers, and avoid squeezing the tick as you pull it out. Do not leave the head embedded, and do not handle the tick. Apply antiseptic to the bite and wash thoroughly. If you develop a rash or any illness within two or three weeks of the bite, see a doctor.

Bears and Mountain Lions

Bear attacks are extremely unlikely anywhere in Texas. Grizzlies have not roamed the state for many decades, and except for a few black bears found in the Guadalupe Mountains, bears of any species had been virtually extinct in Texas since the 1930s. Beginning in the 1980s, however, a small number of black bears began to recolonize the Chisos Mountains. The bears migrated north from the Sierra del Carmen in Mexico, possibly because increased protection in Mexico has led to population growth. These migrants have reproduced and established a small population. The bears are no longer scarce, so you may encounter them. If you do, consider yourself lucky. Very few Texans have ever seen a bear in the wild.

Give any that you see a wide berth, especially those with cubs. If one approaches, yell, make loud noises, wave your arms, and throw rocks. Remain standing to appear large, and don't run away. Check with a ranger for new information before you hike. These recommendations apply only to the bears at Big Bend; other parks and places may have a different situation and advice.

When backpacking, a few precautions will prevent any bear problems. Put all food and other smelly items, such as soap, toothpaste, deodorant, perfume, utensils, water bottles, pots and pans, stoves, and garbage, into the bear-proof boxes found at the primitive campsites in the Chisos Mountains. Leave your packs unzipped to prevent damage to them by a nosy animal. Never cook in your tent or keep food in your tent or sleeping bag. If a bear does somehow take your food, don't even think about trying to get it back. If bears eat human food and become habituated to it, they could be a threat to future visitors and might have to be killed, so do your best to prevent them from obtaining your food. Encounters with bears are unlikely in the desert areas of the park.

The mountain lions in the Chisos Mountains have lost some of their fear of humans after years with no hunting. On rare occasions, hikers have encountered them on the trail. There have been several nonfatal attacks since 1984—not many when you consider how many people hike in the park every year. If you do see a lion, you are among a fortunate few; they are very reclusive. If the lion does not immediately run away, stand your ground, ideally near others to appear large. Do not crouch or play dead. Shout, wave your arms, and throw rocks. Don't act like prey by running away or screaming. Other actions to avoid include hiking alone or at night. Keep small children close to you when hiking.

Check with park rangers for more advice on handling such an encounter.

Snakes

The vast majority of snakes you will encounter (usually you will see none) are nonvenomous. On rare occasions you may encounter a rattlesnake or, even more rarely, a copperhead. Most are not aggressive and will not strike unless stepped on or otherwise provoked. In daytime or cold weather, they are usually holed up under rocks and in cracks. The most likely time to see them is during warm evenings, when they come out to hunt. If you watch your step, don't hike at dusk or at night, and don't put your hands or feet under rocks, ledges, and other places you cannot see, you should never have any problem with snakes. Don't hurt or kill any that you find. Remember, snakes are important predators and are protected in national parks.

If bitten by a venomous snake, get medical help as soon as possible. Treatment methods are controversial and beyond the scope of this book. Fortunately, the majority of bites do not inject a significant amount of venom. Bites by nonvenomous snakes should be kept clean to prevent infection.

Equipment

The most important outdoor equipment is probably your footwear. Hiking boots should be sturdy and comfortable. Lightweight leather and nylon boots are probably adequate for all but the most-rugged trails or when you're carrying heavy packs. Proper clothing, plenty of food and water, and a pack are other necessities. Other vital items for every trip include waterproof matches, rain gear or some sort of emergency shelter, a pocketknife, a signal mirror and whistle, a first-aid kit, a detailed map, and a compass.

Because Big Bend tends to be warm, shorts are popular for hiking. On well-used and maintained trails, shorts do fine. However, on lightly used trails and cross-country routes, be sure to wear long pants. Many plants at Big Bend have thorns and spines to protect themselves from foraging animals. These plants can wreak havoc on uncovered skin. If you do wear shorts, be sure to use sunscreen. Sunscreen and a broad-brimmed hat are vital to protect other parts of the body as well from the strong sun at Big Bend.

In general, all your outdoor equipment should be as light and small as possible. Many excellent books and outdoors shops will help you select the proper boots, tents, sleeping bags, cooking utensils, and other equipment necessary for your hikes.

Getting Lost

Careful use of maps, compasses, GPS units, and hike descriptions should prevent you from ever getting lost. However, if you should become lost or disoriented, immediately stop. Charging around blindly will only worsen the problem. Careful study of the map, compass, GPS, and surrounding landmarks in Big Bend's open country will often reorient you. If you can retrace your route, follow it until you are oriented again. Do not proceed unless you are sure of your location. If you left travel plans with friends or family, rescuers should find you soon if you stay in the expected location.

Often a standard response if lost is to follow a drainage downstream. In most areas of the country, it will eventually lead you to a trail, road, or town. However, at Big Bend, it may well take you deeper into the backcountry instead and cannot be recommended. In addition, that strategy will probably take you farther away from rescuers.

The trails in this guide are well maintained and marked and easy to follow. Read each hike description carefully to determine any potential difficulties in route-finding before you start.

On some hikes, exposed bedrock worn or scratched by the hooves of horses or past mule trains will sometimes help you stay on the route. Trails often follow the easiest terrain. If you have lost the trail, look carefully on the most gentle slopes, the lowest passes, and the flattest benches for signs of the trail. Switchbacks usually indicate a trail; animals do not create them.

If you are lost, the use of signals may help rescuers find you. A series of three flashes or noises is the universal distress signal. Use the whistle or signal mirror. Satellite-linked personal locater beacons (PLBs) have become available in recent years and could be useful in an emergency.

Vehicle Safety

Use care when driving the parks' roads to the trailheads. More serious accidents probably occur on park roads than on the trails. Obey the park speed limits and any warning signs. At night, watch carefully for wildlife on the road.

Most of this guide's hikes have trailheads that can be reached by any car. Some, as noted, require high clearance, and a few may require four-wheel drive, especially in wet weather. Rain or snow can temporarily make even a good road impassable. Before venturing onto Big Bend's dirt roads, you should check with a park ranger at any visitor center or look at the sign boards outside the visitor centers. On the less-traveled back roads, you should carry basic emergency equipment, such as a shovel, chains, water, a spare tire, a jack, blankets, and some extra food and clothing. Make sure that your vehicle is in good operating condition with a full tank of gas.

Theft and vandalism occasionally occur at trailheads, particularly along the river. Park rangers can tell you of any recent problems. Try not to leave valuables in the car at all; if you must, lock them out of sight in the trunk. Ideally, put everything out of sight to give the vehicle an overall empty appearance.

How to Use This Guide

This guide contains the best of the easier trails found in Big Bend National Park. Two included trails, Lost Mine and Window, are harder than the others, but are relatively short and are two of the park's finest trails. This guide offers a wide range of hiking experiences, from an easy 0.25-mile paved route to the 5.6-mile Window Trail. The majority of trailheads in this book are accessible by any type of vehicle. Each description elaborates on any special road conditions. The GPS coordinates for some of the trailheads were measured with a GPS unit on the spot. Others were taken off Google maps, so there may be some slight discrepancies between your measured coordinates and the coordinates given in this book. However, the difference should be too small to create any difficulties in finding the trailheads.

If you are a beginning hiker, don't let the length of some of these trails intimidate you. You don't need to restrict yourself to only the short ones. Most of the longer hikes are very beautiful and rewarding, even if you only go 0.5 mile down the trail.

Although hiking just the trails in this guide may keep you busy for some time, some of the hike descriptions suggest additional nearby routes. As you gain experience, don't be afraid to try them.

This book describes trails scattered widely across Big Bend National Park. The map at the start of this book indicates their locations. Several categories of information describe each hike. The **overview** gives a brief, one-sentence description of the hike. Although the hiking speed of different people varies considerably, we are estimating an approximate hiking speed of 2 miles per hour except for more rugged trails. A hike is loosely classed as a day hike if most reasonably fit people can easily complete it round-trip in one day or less.

The **elevation range** is often the most important factor in determining a hike's difficulty. The two numbers listed are the highest and lowest points reached on the hike. Often, but not always, the trailhead lies at the low point and the end lies at the highest point. With canyon hikes, the numbers are sometimes reversed. Many of the hikes in Big Bend have a fairly steady climb going out and a fairly steady downhill coming back. Some of the hikes have several ups and downs on the way, requiring more elevation gain and effort than the high and low numbers indicate. The Dodson Trail (not included in this guide) is a prime example of this.

Absolute elevation also affects difficulty. At high elevations, lower atmospheric pressure creates "thin air" that requires higher breathing rates and more effort to pull enough oxygen into the lungs. Since most of Big Bend National Park lies at low to moderate elevations, hikers will encounter thin air on only the Lost Mine Trail in this guide. The moderately high elevations encountered on hikes in the Chisos Mountains will require only a little additional effort. Physically fit hikers coming from low-elevation areas should acclimate easily within two or three days.

Except for loop trails, the **distance** and **hiking time** given are usually the one-way mileage and time. There is sometimes some disagreement about distance between maps, published sources, GPS tracks, and trail signs. The distances given in this guide are the author's best estimate using these sources. Some, but not all, have been checked in recent years with a GPS unit. GPS units, however, often overestimate the distance traveled because of positioning error, poor sky visibility, interpolation error, and other problems. Most trails require a return on the same route, so the total mileage and time will usually be double that shown. Some of the trails, such as the Chimneys Trail, can be done one-way if a car shuttle is set up ahead of time and its full length is hiked.

The **difficulty rating** gives a general idea of the physical effort necessary to complete the trail. This rating takes into account the trail's length and condition. Problems in route-finding add to the trail's difficulty. In general, easy trails can be done without difficulty by any person in reasonable physical condition. Moderate trails usually require significant physical effort, but they are not difficult for hikers in good physical condition. Strenuous trails require considerable effort and should only be done by people in very good condition. Most of the trails in this guide, unlike in the comprehensive *Hiking Big Bend* guide, are easy. A very few are moderate or difficult hikes, although not on the level of some of the hikes in the comprehensive guide that are much harder. I've used a different rating scale in this guide to differentiate these hikes from each other.

The **best season** category suggests the ideal time of year for each hike. These are desert parks, so most of the hikes are best done from fall through spring to avoid the worst of the heat. The hikes in the Chisos Mountains in the national park can be done year-round, but an early-morning start is advisable. Even the mountains get pretty hot in summer.

The **schedule** category notes any trail closures during certain times of the year. Usually all of this guide's trails are open year-round.

The **traffic** category is meant to give at least a rough idea of trail usage. Without elaborate hiker counting done over an extended period of time, it is difficult to come up with a purely objective measure of usage. However, on a trail designated as receiving very light use, it is rare to see other hikers. On those designated as having light use, meetings with other hikers are uncommon. On trails marked moderate, you will see at least a few other hikers on most trips. On those marked heavy, you will generally meet several other hiking parties. Realize that trail use is somewhat seasonal. Trail usage overall is lighter at Big Bend during summer, especially on the desert hikes. During Thanksgiving, Christmas vacation, Easter, and college spring break, trail usage increases on all routes.

The **other trail users** category lists other users, such as mountain bikers and equestrians. Mountain bikes are not allowed on any of the national park trails. While equestrians are allowed to use many of the trails in the park, such usage is uncommon and unlikely to be encountered. Dogs are not allowed on any national park trail.

Trail surface describes what your feet will be walking on—from easy footing on paved pathways and boardwalks to more-challenging treks across the gravel and cobbles of desert washes.

The **maps** category gives the names of the United States Geological Survey (USGS) 7.5-minute topographic maps necessary for the trail. These maps are available at the Panther Junction Visitor Center, outdoors shops in Texas, and various online services such as mytopo.com. The National Geographic / Trails Illustrated Big Bend National Park map, available at the visitor centers and outdoors shops, is generally adequate for the trails in this guide. However, it is critical to have the topographic maps and a compass and/or a GPS unit on the less-traveled trails and routes not covered in this guide. Read each description carefully, and talk to park rangers ahead of time to help determine the need for topographic maps. A few errors, particularly trail-routing errors, exist in both the National Geographic / Trails Illustrated map and the topographic maps. Those errors of which the author is aware are mentioned in the trail descriptions.

Some hike entries have **special considerations** to alert you to specific trail hazards or other important information—often, in this book, surrounding the issue of water.

Finding the trailhead provides detailed directions for locating the start of each hike plus its GPS coordinates. With a basic park map, you can easily locate the trailhead from the directions. Distances were measured using a car odometer or mile markers. Realize that different cars will vary slightly in their measurements. Be sure to keep an eye open for the specific signs, junctions, and landmarks mentioned in the directions, not just the mileage or GPS coordinates.

The Hike provides a detailed description of the trail itself, often accompanied by historical, biological, and geological information about the area through which the trail passes. Following this is **Miles and Directions**, a mile-by-mile summary of junctions and major landmarks along the trail. These mileages were generally estimated from the topographic maps or GPS measurements and may be a bit conservative.

Detailed maps accompany each trail description. The map information was taken from USGS topographic maps and national park maps. Use the guidebook's maps in conjunction with the topographic maps and the park map.

The maps in this book that depict a detailed close-up of an area use elevation tints, called hypsometry, to portray relief. Each gray tone represents a range of equal elevation, as shown in the scale key with the map. These maps will give you a good idea of elevation gain and loss. The darker tones are lower elevations; the lighter grays are higher elevations. The lighter the tone, the higher the elevation. Narrow bands of different gray tones spaced closely together indicate steep terrain; wider bands indicate areas of more gradual slope.

After reading the trail descriptions and assessing your desires and abilities, pick a hike that appeals. Then pack your gear and hit the trail!

Park Information
Superintendent
Big Bend National Park
PO Box 129
Big Bend National Park, TX 79834
(432) 477-2251
nps.gov/bibe/index.htm
Camping: recreation.gov
Big Bend National Park requires a seven-day park entrance fee or annual pass for entry.

Map Legend

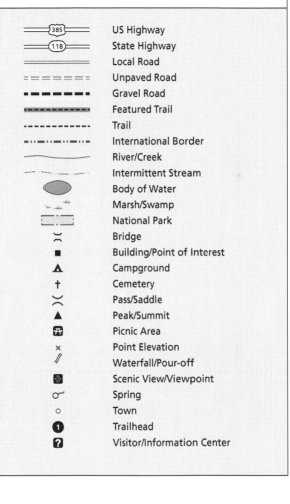

~385~	US Highway
~118~	State Highway
———————	Local Road
– – – – –	Unpaved Road
▪ ▪ ▪ ▪ ▪	Gravel Road
▓▓▓▓▓▓▓	Featured Trail
- - - - - - -	Trail
▪·▪·▪·▪·▪	International Border
～～～	River/Creek
～ - ～ - ～	Intermittent Stream
⬭	Body of Water
	Marsh/Swamp
⎓	National Park
⏝	Bridge
▪	Building/Point of Interest
▲	Campground
†	Cemetery
)(	Pass/Saddle
▲	Peak/Summit
⌷	Picnic Area
×	Point Elevation
∬	Waterfall/Pour-off
⬉	Scenic View/Viewpoint
⚲	Spring
○	Town
❶	Trailhead
❷	Visitor/Information Center

1 Santa Elena Canyon

A day hike into a spectacular canyon cut by the Rio Grande.

Elevation range: 2,160–2,240 feet

Distance: 0.8 mile one way

Hiking time: 30–45 minutes one way

Difficulty: Easy

Best season: Oct through Mar

Schedule: Open year-round

Traffic: Heavy

Other trail users: Hikers only

Trail surface: Dirt and paved path

Maps: USGS Castolon

Finding the trailhead: From Santa Elena Junction, about 13 miles west of Panther Junction on the road to Study Butte and Alpine, drive south about 29 miles all the way to the end of the Ross Maxwell Scenic Drive at Santa Elena Canyon. GPS: N29 10.037' / W103 36.622'

The Hike

This hike takes you into the mouth of one of the three major canyons of the Rio Grande in Big Bend National Park. Because the 1,500-foot-deep canyon is spectacular and the hike is easy, this trail is one of the most popular in the park. Summer temperatures frequently exceed 100°F, so hike early in the morning from about April through October and carry water. Fortunately, there is shade in the canyon. Although there is little net elevation change in the hike, the trail does require a short 80-foot climb up the canyon wall and back down to river level. Colorful interpretive signs highlight the area's geology, history, and plant and animal life along the trail. From the parking area the trail runs through a stand of giant river cane, mesquite, tamarisk, and other plants before dropping into the Terlingua Creek drainage near its confluence with the river. Depending upon recent rainfall, Terlingua Creek may be dry sand, thick mud, or flowing water. Carefully assess conditions and your abilities before attempting to cross. Follow trail signs for the correct crossing location. Crossing at other locations up the creek is dangerous, damages vegetation, and causes erosion. If water levels are too high, do not attempt to cross. Once you cross Terlingua Creek, you immediately climb a fairly steep, paved trail. Rest as needed as you climb and enjoy the views behind you. To the east and southeast, the floodplain of the Rio Grande and the ribbon of river wind through the desert; to the northeast rise the Sierra Quemada and Chisos Mountains.

The cliff on your right as you approach the canyon is the most easterly edge of the Mesa de Anguila, a large mesa in the dry western portion of Big Bend National Park. To your left across the Rio Grande rises the impressive Sierra Ponce, the northern boundary of Mexico and the other canyon wall.

As you reach the trail's high point, you get your first good view of the river in the canyon. From here you descend a series of steep log steps to the narrow river floodplain. The trail follows the river through thick, shady stands of mesquite, cane, and tamarisk, eventually passing under a huge, angular boulder. Just past the boulder the trail winds its way to the wet sand at the river's edge. Several trails twist through the boulders that litter the narrow floodplain, but eventually the river cuts off the path at a sheer canyon wall, blocking further access upstream unless the river is exceptionally low.

Of the three major canyons of the Rio Grande in Big Bend National Park, Santa Elena Canyon is the most frequently boated. Fifteen-hundred-foot walls tower over the river, creating a narrow gorge into which the sun shines for

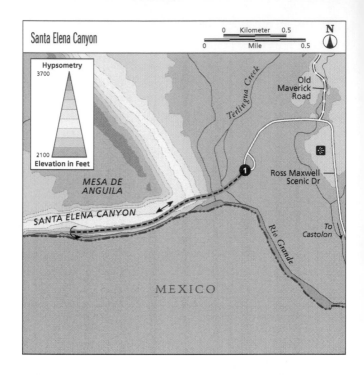

only a short time each day. Although most of the river is fairly flat, the Rockslide—a Class IV/V rapid—adds excitement and challenge to the trip for the many people who float the canyon each year. Although most boaters travel through the canyon on guided trips arranged by outfitters, it is possible for experienced boaters to float Santa Elena Canyon using their own equipment and skills. However, this is not a trip for novice boaters. Be sure to inquire at any park visitor center for more information and to acquire necessary permits. Low water levels caused by excessive Mexican water withdrawals and extended drought have made float trips more difficult in recent years.

Miles and Directions

0.0 Start at the trailhead at the Santa Elena Canyon parking area.

0.8 The trail ends where the river cuts off the riverbank.

2 The Chimneys

A day hike to a prominent rock landmark with petroglyphs in the desert.

Elevation range: 3,190–2,800 feet
Distance: 2.4 miles one way
Hiking time: 1.0–1.5 hours one way
Difficulty: Easy to moderate
Best season: Oct through Mar
Schedule: Open year-round

Traffic: Moderate to the Chimneys; light beyond
Other trail users: Equestrians possible but not likely
Trail surface: Dirt path
Maps: USGS Cerro Castellan, Castolon

Finding the trailhead: From park headquarters at Panther Junction, go about 13 miles west on the road to Alpine and Study Butte. Turn left onto the paved road to Santa Elena Canyon and Castolon. Go about 12.8 miles to the small parking area on the right (west) side of the road, about 1.3 miles beyond the Burro Mesa spur road. A small sign marks the Chimneys Trail. GPS: N29 12.342' / W103 25.409'

The Hike

The tall ridge of rock outcrops known as the Chimneys has been a landmark for hundreds of years. Indian petroglyphs decorate one rock wall, and the remains of small rock shelters used by herders are tucked against the rocks.

This trail is a cool-weather hike. Temperatures can begin to get very hot as early as April 1. The Chimneys at the end of the hike have the only shade. Be sure to carry plenty of water.

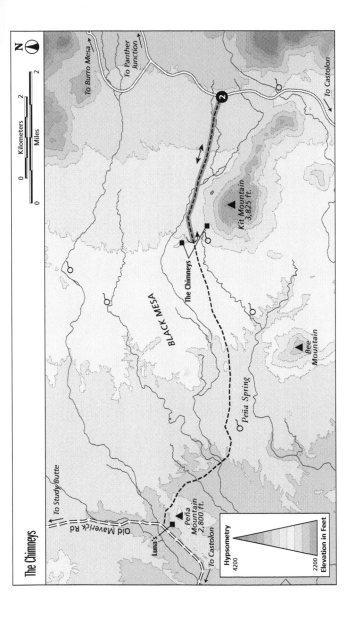

The Chimneys

To Burro Mesa
To Panther Junction
To Castolon

N

Kilometers 0 1 2
Miles 0 1 2

Kit Mountain 3,825 ft.

BLACK MESA

The Chimneys

Bee Mountain

Peña Spring

To Study Butte

Old Maverick Rd

Luna's

Peña Mountain 2,800 ft.

To Castolon

Hypsometry
4200

Elevation in Feet
2200

The trail can be done as a one-way hike to Old Maverick Road, with a shuttle arranged at the other end. However, this description only covers the round-trip day hike as far as the Chimneys, for a total distance of 4.8 miles. The trail is well traveled and clearly visible as far as the Chimneys; beyond, it is much less used and occasionally gets faint. Topographic maps and a compass or GPS unit would be good insurance if you decide to go beyond the Chimneys. The total one-way mileage to Old Maverick Road shown on the trailhead sign is 7.4 miles.

The Chimneys are visible from the trailhead as a long, rocky ridge down the long slope to the west. They appear closer than the 2.4 miles away that they are. The good, easy trail follows a fairly straight route across the desert flats to the Chimneys. The ridge is in sight for virtually all of the hike. The trail slopes slightly downhill for the entire route to the rock formations. Conversely, the entire trail requires a gentle climb on the return trip.

When you reach the Chimneys, you'll see how erosion has carved a narrow ridge into a series of pinnacles and buttes. Indians carved petroglyphs onto a wall of the southernmost rock tower. Please don't disturb or deface them. Some rock shelters surround the same tower. Several unofficial trails wind around the Chimneys allowing additional exploration. Unless you are prepared to continue along the trail to Old Maverick Road, turn around and gently climb back to the trailhead.

Miles and Directions

0.0   Start at the Chimneys trailhead.
2.4   Reach the Chimneys.

3 Lower Burro Mesa Pour-off

A hike to a seasonal waterfall at the southern end of Burro Mesa.

Elevation range: 3,300–3,360 feet

Distance: 0.5 mile one way

Hiking time: About 30 minutes one way

Difficulty: Easy

Best season: Oct through Mar

Schedule: Open year-round

Traffic: Heavy

Other trail users: Equestrians possible but not likely

Trail surface: Dirt path, dry gravel wash

Maps: USGS Cerro Castellan

Finding the trailhead: From the Panther Junction Visitor Center, go west on the park road toward Study Butte and Alpine. Travel about 13 miles to the junction of the road to Santa Elena Canyon and turn left onto the Ross Maxwell Scenic Drive. On your right is Burro Mesa; to your left are the Chisos Mountains. Travel south about 11.5 miles and turn right onto the Burro Mesa spur road. Follow the spur road to its end (1.8 miles). The trailhead is located at the end of the road. GPS: N29 14.042' / W103 24.439'

The Hike

This short trail to a desert pour-off offers much to hikers interested in the geology of Big Bend. To give some perspective, recall the view of the high, rugged peaks of the Chisos Mountains as you drove down to Burro Mesa. The rock exposed in the cliffs here is the same as that found on the top of Emory Peak, the highest point in the park. Burro Mesa is a down-faulted block, a large landmass that dropped along a fault line approximately 26 million years ago. The extent of the displacement is more than 3,000 feet.

Before starting down the trail, hikers should take a moment to look at the rock section exposed in the canyon wall to the left. The darker volcanic rock at the top of the canyon is Burro Mesa Rhyolite. The thick yellow band beneath it is Wasp Spring Flow Breccia. Both of these are members of the South Rim Formation. Underlying the breccia member is an unnamed conglomerate, large boulders of which will be found along the trail. The tall white formation exposed to the right of the trail is volcanic tuff (consolidated ash) of the Chisos Formation.

The first portion of the trail is a well-defined path into the canyon. You first hike to the top of a short slope where the trail descends into a dry wash. By looking up into the canyon ahead, you can see a small pour-off. This is not the final destination, however. Follow the trail down into and across the wash. The trail passes through a dense thicket of guayacan and enters the dry wash again. At this point the trail is no longer a well-defined path. A line of rocks directs hikers into the drainage opening to the right. Continuing up this gravel-floored wash, you pass several healthy stands of Texas persimmon, which in late summer can be filled with small black persimmons and large wasps feasting on them. About halfway up the wash on the right, a large Mexican buckeye offers hikers a shady spot to sit and rest. Beyond this point, the wash continues up the canyon and turns to the left. The Burro Mesa Pour-off comes into view, high above.

The pour-off is a long, narrow chute that drains Javelina Wash from the canyon in the cliffs above. The dark, polished rock that is exposed for most of the length of the chute is Burro Mesa Rhyolite. The contact between the rhyolite and

Lower Burro Mesa Pour-off; Upper Burro Mesa

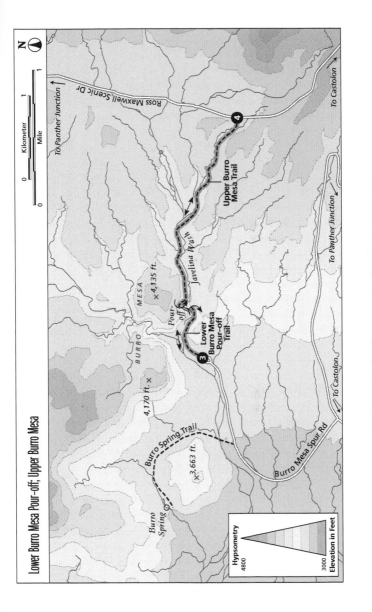

Hypsometry

4800

3000

Elevation in Feet

N

0   Kilometer   1

0   Mile   1

To Panther Junction

Ross Maxwell Scenic Dr

To Castolon

Upper Burro Mesa Trail

Javelina Wash

Pour-off

MESA

× 4,135 ft.

BURRO

× 4,170 ft.

Lower Burro Mesa Pour-off Trail

3

4

To Castolon

To Panther Junction

Burro Mesa Spur Rd

Burro Spring Trail

× 3,663 ft.

Burro Spring

the Wasp Spring Breccia is seen quite easily in the ledges just above your head. Usually the chute is dry, but the extent of the cut testifies to the powerful torrent of water that can be generated after heavy summer rains fall on the upper reaches of Burro Mesa and the western slopes of the Chisos Mountains.

Do not try to climb up to the pour-off. Cliffs and steep slopes with loose rubble make ascents hazardous. It can be reached by following the Upper Burro Mesa (Top of Burro Mesa Pour-off) Trail found elsewhere in this guide. Although this walk is short, it can be very hot in summer. Plan to hike it early in the day during the warm months. Be wary of flooding during and after heavy rains.

Another nearby easy hike is the Burro Spring Trail. Its marked trailhead lies about 0.7 mile back along the Burro Mesa spur road. It's a 1.2-mile one-way hike to a small, but lush desert spring.

Miles and Directions

0.0   Start at the trailhead.

0.1   The trail descends into and crosses a dry wash.

0.2   The trail enters the wash again. Follow rock alignment into a big drainage to the right, and follow the wash upstream to the pour-off.

0.5   Arrive at the pour-off.

4 Upper Burro Mesa

A hike through some narrow, rocky gorges to the lip of a high, dry waterfall.

See map on page 37.

Elevation range: 3,990–3,460 feet
Distance: 1.8 miles one way
Hiking time: 1–1.5 hours one way
Difficulty: Moderate
Best season: Oct through Mar

Schedule: Open year-round
Traffic: Light to moderate
Other trail users: Equestrians possible but not likely
Trail surface: Dirt path and sand, gravel, and cobbles of dry desert wash
Maps: USGS Cerro Castellan

Finding the trailhead: From the Santa Elena Junction about 13 miles west of Panther Junction on the road to Study Butte and Alpine, drive south on the Ross Maxwell Scenic Drive toward Castolon and Santa Elena Canyon. The trailhead is located at the marked paved pullout on the right at about 6.9 miles. GPS: N29 13.775' / W103 22.664'

The Hike

This trail is known now as the Upper Burro Mesa Trail, although it was once sometimes called the Top of Burro Mesa Pour-off Trail. The trail to the top of the Burro Mesa Pour-off is relatively easy physically, but it does require some route-finding skill. A topographic map and compass and/or a GPS unit would be good insurance for this hike. Most of the hike follows desert washes where there is no formal trail, and rock cairns may wash away in floods. Although the route is primitive, most of the walking is easy, except for a few rock scrambles early in the hike and at the very end. Although canyon walls create some shade, especially toward the end of the hike, this is a very hot walk in summer. Take plenty of water.

The trail trends steadily downward, mostly at a gentle grade, through a series of desert washes all the way to the top of the pour-off. The pour-off is a high, dry desert waterfall that drops precipitously from the canyon that the trail follows into a rugged lower canyon. In flash floods, the waterfall and canyon can become a raging torrent, so this hike should be avoided in stormy weather.

The trail, clearly visible at first, drops down into a small, grassy valley below the parking pullout. It follows the valley downstream a short distance and then drops into a gravel-and-rock wash. The valley narrows into a rocky canyon, requiring some rock scrambling down the wash. After about 0.75 mile a large tributary joins the canyon from the right. Note carefully the proper canyon for your return hike. The canyon broadens and the grade lessens below the confluence. Another, even larger wash, Javelina Wash, joins from the right in another 0.25 mile. Again note your return route. These two side washes are the most likely points of confusion on the return hike. However, if you should take one by accident, it's no problem; they both end up on the highway just north of the trailhead.

After the Javelina Wash confluence, the wash becomes large. Follow it the rest of the way downstream to the pour-off. The canyon walls slowly close in and get higher and higher. There's even an arch on the right. Just before the main pour-off at the end, the canyon turns into a slot canyon—scenic, but a poor place to be in a flood. Use care climbing down the small pour-off in the slot canyon; it's slick. Just beyond, at the main pour-off, the canyon ends abruptly where it drops off into space. Far below, you may see people hiking up to the base of the pour-off from the Lower Burro Mesa Pour-off Trail, found elsewhere in this guide. However, because of the tall cliff, you will need to hike back the same way.

Miles and Directions

0.0 Start at the Upper Burro Mesa trailhead.

1.0 The trail joins Javelina Wash.

1.8 Arrive at the Upper Burro Mesa Pour-off.

5 Sam Nail Ranch

An easy walk through an old ranch site below Burro Mesa.

Elevation range: 3,620–3,650 feet
Distance: 0.5-mile loop
Hiking time: About 30 minutes
Difficulty: Easy
Best season: All (Start early in summer.)

Schedule: Open year-round
Traffic: Heavy
Other trail users: Hikers only
Trail surface: Dirt path
Maps: USGS The Basin

Finding the trailhead: From the Santa Elena Junction about 13 miles west of Panther Junction on the road to Study Butte and Alpine, drive south on the Ross Maxwell Scenic Drive toward Castolon and Santa Elena Canyon. The trailhead lies at the large, paved pullout on the right after 3.4 miles. GPS: N29 16.769' / W103 22.119'

The Hike

This short, well-maintained trail loops through the old Sam Nail Ranch site. Sam Nail and his younger brother, Jim, moved to the valley between the western slope of the Chisos Mountains and Burro Mesa in 1916. With little outside help, they dug a well and built a one-story adobe house above Cottonwood Creek at the base of Burro Mesa. The home had a concrete floor, wooden viga-and-cane ceiling, and sheet-metal roof. With milk cows, chickens, cattle, a garden, and fruit trees, they were relatively self-sufficient. In 1918 Sam married Nena Burnam, whose family lived nearby at Government Spring.

The Nails owned several sections and leased more for their ranching activities. After they left, nature began to reclaim the site. Rains have slowly melted away much of the soft adobe walls of the house, and desert plants have taken over the yard and garden. The park still maintains a windmill at the ranch; its waters sustain a tiny oasis of walnuts, pecans, willows, and even a fig tree.

The trail heads west, slightly downhill, from the parking lot and forks into a loop in 100 yards or so. Go right and pass an old, ruined windmill that is leaning over precariously in a short distance. The trail then drops down into a thicket of small trees in the floodplain of Cottonwood Creek. A very short, unofficial side trail on the right leads to an old chicken coop and the creek. A few cottonwoods line the creek, where small amounts of water sometimes flow, depending on rainfall.

From the thicket, the main trail leads into a grove of larger trees surrounding the working windmill. The wind slowly pumps up a small flow of water that nourishes the surrounding trees and plants. Even such a small flow makes a tremendous biological difference in such dry desert country. Relax on a bench in the cool shade and listen to the sounds of the creaking windmill mixed with plentiful birdcalls. You may see cardinals, summer tanagers, house finches, mocking-birds, varied buntings, and many other species.

From the windmill, continue around the loop on the main trail. Resist the urge to take a shortcut by the windmill to the old house ruins in this heavily visited spot. The old adobe walls of the ranch house lie on the left only a short distance up the hill on the main trail. From the old house, continue the rest of the way around the loop and back to the parking lot.

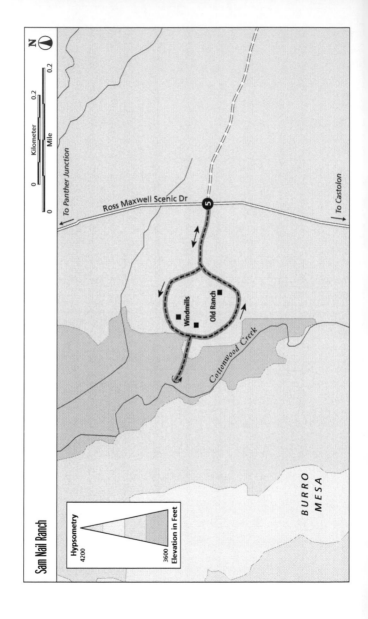

Sam Nail Ranch

Hypsometry

4200

3600

Elevation in Feet

N

0   Kilometer   0.2

0   Mile   0.2

To Panther Junction

Ross Maxwell Scenic Dr

5

To Castolon

Windmills

Old Ranch

Cottonwood Creek

BURRO
MESA

Miles and Directions

0.0 Start at the Sam Nail Ranch parking area. Go right at the beginning of the loop.

0.25 Reach a working windmill.

0.5 Arrive back at the Sam Nail Ranch parking area.

6 Grapevine Hills

A day hike into the jumbled boulder pile of the Grapevine Hills, ending at a stone window.

Elevation range: 3,240–3,480 feet

Distance: 1.0 mile one way

Hiking time: About 30 minutes one way

Difficulty: Easy

Best season: Oct through Mar

Schedule: Open year-round

Traffic: Moderate

Other trail users: Hikers only

Trail surface: Dirt path, sand, gravel, and cobbles of a desert wash, and bare rock

Maps: USGS Grapevine Hills

Special considerations: There is no water along the trail.

Finding the trailhead: Drive west from Panther Junction headquarters about 3 miles on the road to Study Butte. Just after passing the Basin turnoff on the left, look for the sign for the Grapevine Hills Road on the right. Follow the Grapevine Hills Road for about 6.5 miles; the trailhead will be on the right. It is a small gravel parking area with a trailhead sign. Parking at this trailhead is limited. If you have a large vehicle, you may not find adequate space, especially during busy times such as college spring break, Christmas, or Thanksgiving.

This is a gravel road, and the last 2–3 miles can get a little rough; it's best to use a high-clearance vehicle. At a minimum, use a small SUV like a Subaru Forester, Ford Escape, or the like. Check on road conditions at a park visitor center before heading to the trailhead. GPS: N29 24.624' / W 103 12.459'

The Hike

The Grapevine Hills Trail is a relatively easy 1-mile walk, most of it on relatively flat terrain. You will be walking in and out of a sandy wash for the first 0.75 mile, with a gradual rise in elevation. For the last 0.25 mile, the trail becomes more strenuous as it climbs up a short but steep rocky slope before ending at a large balanced rock perched overhead between two rock pinnacles. That last steep slope has a lot of loose pebbles, making it a bit treacherous. Use care there; the park has had to rescue people who have fallen and broken ankles or had other injuries on that slope.

Although there are occasional bits of shade in the lee of boulders and pinnacles, this is usually a hot hike from April through September. If you hike during the hot season, be sure to get an early start. There is no water on the trail, so carry plenty any time of year.

The obvious trail heads south-southeast into the small canyon leading out of the back side of the parking area. The first 0.75 mile of the trail follows a desert wash upstream through the canyon and winds in and out of the sandy streambed and across benches (relatively level areas of land) above the wash. Although there are several branches of the wash (it is called a braided channel), do not worry about following the wrong branch. The branches split and then rejoin later. Footprints of hikers before you typically lead up several of the branches. The soft sand of the wash gets a little tiring for walking, so try to stay on benches when the trail is there.

The wash is lined with typical desert vegetation. In addition to creosote bush, cenizo, skeleton-leaf goldeneye, and acacias, you will also see guayacan and persimmon in abundance. The wash is bounded by the scenic terrain of the Grapevine Hills; eroded rocks tower over you on either side of the canyon as you walk along.

The Grapevine Hills formed when a mass of granitic rock weathered and eroded into unusual shapes. The rocks are igneous in origin and were created when molten rock intruded into overlying sedimentary rock. The magma cooled and hardened into a large dome-shaped body called a laccolith. Eventually erosion stripped away the softer overlying sedimentary rock and exposed the granite that we see today. Most of the giant granite boulders in the area were once rectangular and blocky, but as water seeped into fractures in the rock, the corners eroded more quickly than the sides, producing rounded shapes. This is called spheroidal weathering and is much in evidence all along the trail.

The Grapevine Hills granite is composed of a mixture of minerals, including quartz, feldspar, and mica. The weaker minerals erode faster, creating a rough surface on exposed rocks. Shallow pits are often formed where rainwater pools rather than running off the rock. Chemical reactions cause some of the minerals in the rock to slowly dissolve, creating a pit on the rock surface. Note the wide variety of rock shapes as you hike the trail.

At the upper end of the wash, the trail begins to climb steeply upward and out of the small canyon to a low saddle. At the saddle the trail turns sharply right and follows the ridge upward to the right. The route here winds through rock formations and is a bit confusing. Look for several small signs and metal fence posts to help guide you. It is only 100 yards or so to the arch at the end of the trail, but it is a steep climb among the rocks. You may need to use both hands and feet at some spots. Once at the balanced rock window, the view opens up toward the south and southeast; the most prominent feature is Nugent Mountain, about 10 miles away. The trail ends here; to return to the parking area, retrace your steps.

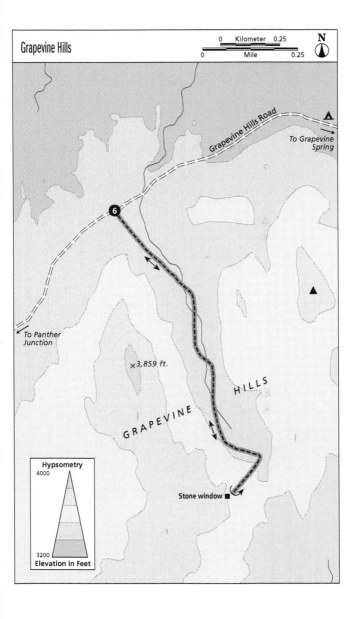

Grapevine Hills

0   Kilometer   0.25
0   Mile   0.25

N

Grapevine Hills Road

To Grapevine Spring

6

To Panther Junction

×3,859 ft.

GRAPEVINE   HILLS

Stone window ■

Hypsometry
4000

3200
Elevation in Feet

Miles and Directions

0.0 Start at the trailhead on the Grapevine Hills Road.

0.75 The trail climbs out of the wash to a saddle.

1.0 Arrive at the stone window.

7 Window View

An introductory day hike that winds through a mountain grassland to a spectacular view of the Window.

Elevation range: 5,370–5,400 feet
Distance: 0.25-mile loop
Hiking time: About 30 minutes
Difficulty: Very easy; barrier-free
Best season: All (Start early in summer.)

Schedule: Open year-round
Traffic: Heavy
Other trail users: Hikers only
Trail surface: Paved
Maps: USGS The Basin

Finding the trailhead: The trail starts in the Basin at the main trailhead located near the Basin store, visitor center, and lodge. From the store, follow the sidewalk downhill to the west to the main trailhead signs. Look for the paved Window View Trail (not the dirt Window Trail) at the trailhead junctions. GPS: N29 16.208' / W103 18.059'

The Hike

This easy, paved loop walk winds through a mountain grassland to a spectacular view of the Window. The pinyon pine, juniper, and oak passed along the way once extended across the desert and down to the Rio Grande. Climatic changes during the last 15,000 years caused the area to become warmer and drier, leaving forests only at higher elevations where they can still survive because of the additional moisture and cooler temperatures found there.

Near the start of the trail, you encounter a plaque commemorating Stephen T. Mather. An influential and wealthy Chicago industrial leader, Mather served as the first director

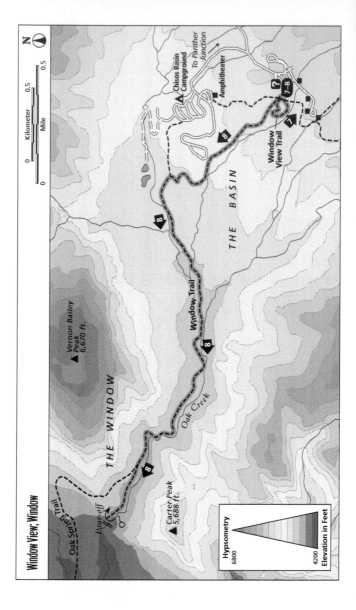

Window View; Window

of the National Park Service from 1917 to 1929. He led the drive establishing the National Park Service, formulated policy, and developed the organization required to manage the national park system.

At the midpoint, relax on a bench and enjoy the view of the Window, the V-shaped opening in the mountains on the western horizon. Precipitation falling in the Basin drains through the Window to the desert below. Because no reliable water source exists in the Basin, all potable water for the Basin's visitor facilities comes from Oak Spring, in the desert below the Window. Large pumps push the water 1,500 feet higher in elevation via a pipeline through the Window to the Basin development. Because water is such a scarce commodity at Big Bend, be sure to use it wisely during your visit.

Parts of the small towns of Study Butte and Terlingua can be seen in the distance through the Window. On a clear day, peaks in Big Bend Ranch State Park and the Sierra Rica of Mexico stand visible on the horizon, 35 miles away. The view covers a broad sweep of the vast terrain of the Big Bend. At sunset, the walk offers one of the best sights in Texas. Clouds light up gold, scarlet, and orange as the sun sinks below the horizon. As the colors fade into dusk, the distant lights of Terlingua and Study Butte blink into life, welcoming the cool night.

Miles and Directions

0.0 Start at the Basin trailhead.

0.25 Loop ends at the Basin trailhead.

8 Window

A day hike from the main Basin trailhead to the Window in the Chisos Mountains or a day hike from the Basin Campground.

See map on page 52.

Elevation range: 5,400–4,400 feet
Distance: 2.8 miles one way
Hiking time: 1.5–2 hours one way
Difficulty: Moderately strenuous

Best season: All (Start early in summer.)
Schedule: Open year-round
Traffic: Heavy
Other trail users: Hikers only
Trail surface: Dirt path
Maps: USGS The Basin

Finding the trailhead: The trail starts in the Basin at the main trailhead, located near the Basin store, visitor center, and lodge. From the store, follow the sidewalk downhill to the west to the main trailhead sign. Look for the Window Trail (not Window View Trail) signs at the trailhead junctions. GPS: N29 16.208' / W103 18.059'

The Hike

The Window Trail leads to the Window, a large rock canyon cutting through the Chisos Mountains rim that allows drainage from the Basin. It frames panoramic desert vistas and enhances spectacular scarlet sunsets. The hike offers good wildlife viewing opportunities and an introduction to the geology and plant life of the Chisos Mountains, along with great mountain scenery. Near the end of the Window Trail, a side trail to Oak Spring leads 0.25 mile to a high perch offering outstanding views of the desert far below. The hike is pleasant most of the year. Summers can be fairly hot, so the hike is usually most comfortable in early morning or late afternoon at that time of year. As you would on other Big Bend hikes, take water, a hat, and sunscreen.

The well-maintained trail descends for its entire length, sometimes fairly steeply in the upper sections. Remember, it may be easy to hike down to the Window, but the underestimated return requires a significant climb, uphill all the way. Be sure to take plenty of water and make sure you can do the harder uphill return hike, particularly when the weather is hot. Because of the uphill return, park rangers have to help people more on this trail than on any other in the park. The last 0.25 mile or so of the trail lies in a slickrock canyon, where footing becomes more difficult. There are rock steps, wet slippery surfaces, and sometimes a short wade across a seasonal creek.

From the main Basin trailhead, the trail begins descending almost immediately, passing through scattered oaks, pines, and junipers. A little more than 0.5 mile down the trail, a spur on the right goes to the campground trailhead. The trail heads west from the spur, traversing the Basin, an eroded bowl that lies some 2,500 feet below the surrounding peaks. Discoveries of American Indian artifacts, refuse heaps, baking pits, campsites, and rock art indicate sporadic human occupation in the Basin for thousands of years. Early ranching pioneers used the slopes of the Basin for grazing livestock.

Volcanoes and underground igneous activity created the peaks surrounding the Basin. Beginning about 38 million years ago, two volcanoes spewed vast quantities of ash and lava, while underneath, molten rock squeezed into the bedrock from below, causing the ancestral Chisos Mountains to rise.

After eons of erosion, the resistant rhyolite magma intrusions remain as Ward Mountain, Carter Peak (the sharply pointed peak on the Window's left side), Vernon Bailey Peak (the rounded mountain on the Window's right), and Pulliam Bluff. Towering Casa Grande, Toll Mountain, and Emory Peak, opposite the Window, consist of lava flows and ash beds. Water, wind, heat, and cold have weathered the heavily fissured ridges surrounding the Basin into distinctive pinnacles, spires, and the famous silhouette of the Window.

After a fairly open stretch of about 1 mile or so, the trail reaches wooded Oak Creek. Be sure to watch closely for wildlife in the underbrush. The small Sierra del Carmen white-tailed deer browse on and off throughout the day, while the piglike collared peccary, or javelina, roots and forages for succulent vegetation. Look for rock squirrels stashing acorns and pine nuts on steep rock faces. Your chance of seeing a gray fox, ringtail, or even a mountain lion improves in the evening or early morning. Black bears are fairly common in this area, especially in the fall, when they feed on nuts of the Mexican pinyon pine.

The combination of cacti and century plants—more characteristic of the desert—growing near oak trees, evergreen sumac, and other mountain species may seem odd. However, at the end of the most recent glacial period, a cool, moist climate was replaced by today's warmer and drier conditions. Consequently, desert-adapted plants have taken over the park's lower elevations and infiltrated partway into the mountains. Species adapted to the former climatic conditions withdrew to the cooler, moister, and more hospitable mountains. Pines, oaks, and junipers that once lived at lower altitude have now become dominant plants in the Basin and higher. Look for several of these relict species, or holdovers from the past, including the Mexican droop-ing juniper and Mexican pinyon pine, along the trail. You may see other distinctive mountain plants, including Texas madrone, mountain mahogany, mountain sage, Mexican buckeye, evergreen sumac, and palo prieto, also known as vauquelinia.

As the trail descends, it leaves the Basin and enters a narrow rock canyon formed by Oak Creek as it carved its way through the Window. Depending on rainfall, a spring sometimes surfaces in the canyon bottom and creates a small flowing stream. Near the end of the trail, the Oak Spring Trail forks off to the right. It climbs above the pour-off, affording great desert views in about 0.25 mile. It then descends around the pour-off to Oak Spring and beyond. Soon after passing the junction, the improved dirt trail ends. Beyond here, the trail follows sections of bare rock and stone steps a short distance down to the trail's end at the top of the Window Pour-off. If rainfall has been adequate, a small stream tumbles down over small cascades through a polished rock course alongside the trail. Do not approach the top of the pour-off too closely; slippery, wet rocks make footing treacherous. A fall would be fatal.

As the only drainage system for the Basin, Oak Creek and its tributaries channel all rain and snowmelt through the Window, the sole gap in the Basin rim. Although the Basin receives only about 15 inches of precipitation annually, sum-mer thundershowers can turn the rock gorge at the end of the Window Trail into a raging torrent in less than an hour. Rushing water carries pebbles and debris through this nar-row defile to plummet 220 feet over the Window Pour-off to the desert below. Be wary here during stormy weather; a flash flood could wash you over the lip. As the years go by,

storms will continue to scour the slopes of the Basin, eroding
it deeper and deeper.

Miles and Directions

0.0   Start at the Basin trailhead.

0.6   Campground spur trail junction. Stay left and continue
downhill.

2.5   Oak Spring Trail junction. Stay left, downstream.

2.8   Arrive at the Window Pour-off.

Option: Alternatively, the hike can be started at the trailhead
between campsites 49 and 51 in the lower loop of the Basin
Campground. Because parking is limited in the campground
loop, park in the amphitheater lot across the road from the
campground and follow the Window Trail signs through the
campground to the trailhead. This option is 2.2 miles one
way.

9 Lost Mine

A day hike to high mountain overlooks with some of the best views in the park.

Elevation range: 5,750–6,850 feet
Distance: 2.4 miles one way
Hiking time: 1.5–2 hours one way
Difficulty: Moderately strenuous

Best season: All (Start early in summer.)
Schedule: Open year-round
Traffic: Heavy
Other trail users: Hikers only
Trail surface: Dirt path
Maps: USGS The Basin

Finding the trailhead: From Panther Junction, drive 3 miles west toward Study Butte. Turn left onto the Basin road and drive 5.4 miles to the large parking area on the left at Panther Pass. This trailhead often fills up, particularly Nov through Apr. Start your hike early or late in the day to be able to park. GPS: N29 16.466' / W103 17.201'

The Hike

The Lost Mine Trail is one of the most popular in the park. Most hikers in good shape can do the round-trip in 3 to 4 hours. For those without the time or ability to hike to the South Rim, this trail is an excellent substitute. People with even less time or energy may elect to hike only the relatively easy first mile of the trail; on clear days this provides beautiful views of Juniper Canyon and south into Mexico.

Between 1940 and 1942, Civilian Conservation Corps (CCC) crews built this trail for the new Big Bend National Park, authorized in 1935 and established in 1944. Look for evidence of their skilled craftsmanship in the stonework of the old walls and culverts found along the path. The surface of the Lost Mine Trail is rocky and well worn, with rock and log water bars scattered along the route. Water bars are small ridges built across the trail that channel water off the trail to limit erosion.

From the parking area, the trail ascends gradually through juniper, oak, and pinyon pine forest along the base of Casa Grande Peak. Do not let the steep first 100 feet or so scare you away. At a little less than 1 mile the trail reaches a saddle that looks out over Juniper Canyon and far south into Mexico. From this vantage point you will have views of Casa Grande to the west and Toll Mountain and the East Rim of the Chisos to the south and southwest.

Listen for the loud, raucous call of the Mexican jay; you might see a flash of bright blue as it flies across your path. This is also a good place for the black-crested titmouse—a small, crested bird whose plaintive call of "peter, peter, peter" is easily identified.

After the saddle, the trail climbs more steeply up a few switchbacks then flattens out temporarily on an open hillside of stipa grass, pinyon pine, and juniper. The trail quickly begins climbing steeply again. Views of Juniper Canyon continue. The trail then narrows, and woods of pinyon pine and oak close in. More switchbacks rapidly add elevation, and good views resume to the south and west. In the midst of the switchbacks, you can look west and see the Chisos Basin Campground and the Window.

On the last couple of switchbacks, the trail gets very steep and rocky. Log and rock steps and exposed bedrock in this stretch can be slippery if wet. To most hikers' relief, the trail abruptly levels off at the top of the ridge. Most of the last 0.5 mile along the exposed ridge is easy. Walk all the way

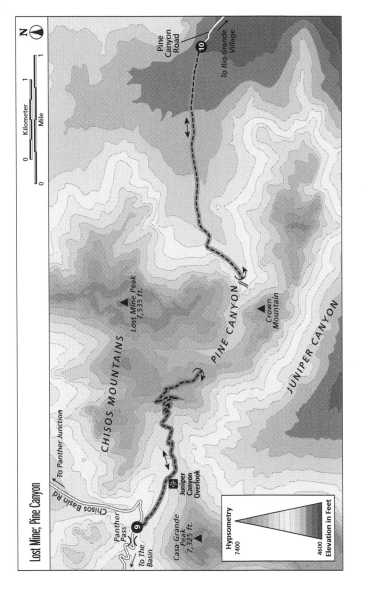

Lost Mine; Pine Canyon

N

Hypsometry
7400
4600
Elevation in Feet

0 Kilometer 1
0 Mile 1

To The Basin
To Panther Junction
Panther Pass
Chisos Basin Rd
9
Casa Grande Peak 7,325 ft.
Juniper Canyon Overlook
CHISOS MOUNTAINS
Lost Mine Peak 7,535 ft.
PINE CANYON
Crown Mountain
JUNIPER CANYON
Pine Canyon Road
10
To Rio Grande Village

to the end for the best views of Pine Canyon (below, to the left) and the Sierra del Carmen in Mexico (on the eastern horizon). On the right, sheer cliffs tumble down into Juniper Canyon, far below. The East Rim of the Chisos Mountains towers over the far side of the broad canyon, and the distinctive pointed summit of Elephant Tusk rises above the desert to the south.

Just northeast, across Pine Canyon, lies Lost Mine Peak, one of the highest summits in the Chisos. The peak was named for an old legend. Supposedly, at certain times of the year the rising sun shines on the entrance of a rich mine developed by the old Spaniards. Unfortunately, the Chisos Mountains are not geologically predisposed to such mineralization, making the legend probably little more than a fanciful story. The treasures here are more spiritual than material.

Miles and Directions

0.0   Start at the Panther Pass trailhead.

0.8   Reach Juniper Canyon overlook.

2.4   The trail ends.

10 Pine Canyon

A day hike through a sotol grassland into a shaded Chisos Mountains canyon.

See map on page 61.

Elevation range: 4,820–5,800 feet
Distance: 2.0 miles one way
Hiking time: About 1 hour one way
Difficulty: Moderate
Best season: All (Start early in summer.)

Schedule: Open year-round
Traffic: Moderate
Other trail users: Hikers only
Trail surface: Dirt path
Maps: USGS Panther Junction, The Basin
Special considerations: Check on road conditions at park headquarters before you begin.

Finding the trailhead: From park headquarters at Panther Junction, take the road to Rio Grande Village. About 5 miles down the road, turn right onto the dirt Glenn Spring Road. After following this road for about 2 miles, turn right onto Pine Canyon Road. Follow it to the trailhead at its end. A high-clearance vehicle is usually needed for Glenn Spring and Pine Canyon Roads. GPS: N29 16.043' / W103 13.692'

The Hike

This trail provides expansive views of high-desert grasslands and the drier desert below before leading into a densely wooded canyon of the Chisos Mountains. Because Lloyd Wade once had a ranch here, the canyon was called Wade Canyon at one time. The trail crosses part of an ancient collapsed volcano, or caldera. The hike is hot in summer, but still considerably cooler than the desert lowlands. Get an early start during the warm months of the year, and carry lots of water. Plenty of shade on the last 0.6 mile makes the hike pleasant even on hot days.

The trail follows an old dirt road, a continuation of Pine Canyon Road, steadily uphill through a sotol-dotted grassland. The canyon narrows as you climb to the west toward the mountains. The old road ends as the trail turns toward the southwest and enters a more narrow and sheltered section of Pine Canyon. The path enters thick woodland and winds among oaks, junipers, pinyon pines, and even Arizona pines. Texas madrones, smooth white- to pinkish-barked evergreen trees, are common in this protected canyon. Reduced exposure to sun and wind allows trees and other plants to thrive here.

The trail climbs steadily up the canyon and ends at the base of a 200-foot-high pour-off. After heavy rains it can be a good waterfall, but most of the time it only drips at most. This is one of the few places in the park where columbine, a beautiful yellow-flowered plant, grows; be careful not to step on vegetation in the pour-off area. Relax in the shade and enjoy one of the lushest areas in the park. Because the canyon is small and delicate, camping is not allowed here.

Miles and Directions

0.0 Start at the trailhead. The trail follows an old dirt road west toward the mountains.

1.4 The trail enters a shaded canyon, where old road ends.

2.0 The trail ends at the base of a pour-off.

11 Ernst Tinaja

A day hike up a dry wash to Ernst Tinaja, a natural rock water hole.

Elevation range: 2,170–2,320 feet
Distance: 0.5 mile one way
Hiking time: About 20 minutes one way
Difficulty: Easy
Best season: Oct through Mar
Schedule: Open year-round
Traffic: Moderate

Other trail users: Equestrians possible but not likely
Trail surface: Sand, gravel, bedrock, and cobbles of dry desert wash
Maps: USGS Roys Peak
Special considerations: Check road conditions with a park ranger before beginning your trip.

Finding the trailhead: From Panther Junction take the road to Rio Grande Village. At about 18 miles turn left (north) onto Old Ore Road. After about 4.5 miles turn right onto 0.5-mile-long Ernst Tinaja Spur Road; the trailhead is at the end of the road past the primitive campsite. Parking for the trailhead is available at the turnaround at the end of the spur road, just past the primitive campsite. Old Ore Road and the Ernst Tinaja Spur are primitive dirt roads that usually require high clearance and sometimes four-wheel drive. GPS: N29 15.171' / W103 01.052'

The Hike

Ernst Tinaja is reached by simply walking up the dry wash for about 0.5 mile. The word "tinaja" (pronounced ti-NA-ha) is Spanish for "large earthen jar" and refers to a basin-shaped water hole, usually carved into bedrock by natural erosion. These water holes are important sources of water in the canyons and rocky terrain of the Chihuahuan Desert. Insects, birds, snakes, frogs, deer, mountain lions, bears, and other creatures all depend on water sources like Ernst Tinaja for survival. Because of that, be careful never to contaminate any water source with soap, sunscreen, or other pollutants.

The water hole creates a welcome oasis, hidden away in the dry, inhospitable Dead Horse Mountains. It is hot in summer, but the canyon walls provide some shade. The permanent supply of water supports a tiny, isolated community of plants and animals, where small-scale life-and-death struggles are played out every day. A small spring may add water to the tinaja, because it never seems to dry up. The sides of the tinaja are very smooth and often covered with slick algae. When the water level gets low, animals can drown in the tinaja because they are unable to climb back out.

The canyon containing Ernst Tinaja cuts through Cuesta Carlota, the western edge of the Dead Horse Mountains. As you wander up the wash, note the tilted layers of bedrock emerging from the blanket of stream gravel. The canyon walls expose tilted and folded rock layers with intricate patterns of red, orange, purple, and gray. Because of the huge faults and uplifts that created these mountains, the originally flat-lying beds now slope steeply to the west.

Unlike the Chisos Mountains, which were formed by the intrusion of molten igneous rock, the Dead Horse and Sierra del Carmen ranges are enormous blocks of limestone that were uplifted along faults. The Mesa de Anguila on the western side of the park was formed by a similar uplift, leaving the majority of the park in a sunken block of the earth's crust between two raised mountain ranges.

As you continue up the wash, you are walking back in geologic time toward older and older strata. Watch how the rock beds change as you approach the tinaja, becoming thinner and changing from relatively pure whitish limestone to colorful shale and limestone. The fossils of large clams and other marine creatures show that these beds were originally deposited on the ocean floor about 90 million years ago, during the Cretaceous period. Geologists have named these rocks the Boquillas Formation. This lowermost part of the Boquillas Formation is further distinguished as the Ernst Member, named for Ernst Tinaja.

At the tinaja, another rock formation, the Buda Limestone, is exposed. Ernst Tinaja is a large depression carved by erosion into the top of the Buda Limestone. This grayish-white rock is composed of thick, massive beds of limestone, in sharp contrast to the thin, colorful beds of the overlying Boquillas Formation. This dramatic change in rock strata indicates a gap in the geologic record called an unconformity. The unconformity indicates a period of erosion or nondeposition of sediments that may have lasted for millions of years. During this time conditions changed in the ancient sea, changing the ways in which the rock layers were deposited and explaining the different appearance of the two rock formations.

As the thin clay-rich beds of the Boquillas Formation were deposited on the uneven, eroded surface of the Buda Limestone, they may have slipped and slumped occasionally. This is probably what caused the intricate folds you see near the tinaja.

You may continue up the canyon above the tinaja for a limited distance before the way is blocked by huge boulders and steep slickrock. If rain threatens, do not stay in the canyon. Flash floods occasionally sweep down, washing away everything in their path.

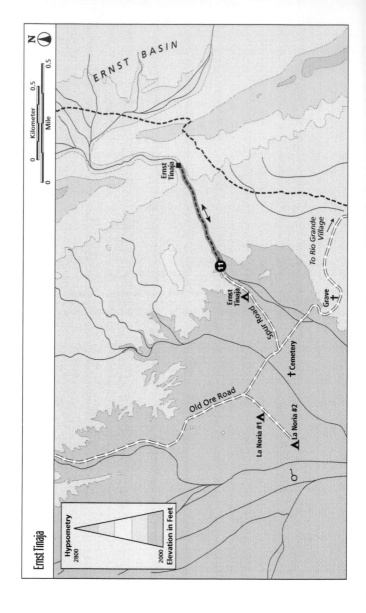

Ernst Tinaja

Miles and Directions

0.0   Start at the trailhead at the end of Ernst Tinaja Spur Road.

0.1   Reach rock outcrops (Boquillas Formation) in a dry wash.

0.5   Arrive at Ernst Tinaja.

12 Hot Springs

A day hike past historic buildings and a large hot spring on the banks of the Rio Grande.

Elevation range: 1,840–1,960 feet
Distance: 1.0-mile loop
Hiking time: About 30 minutes
Difficulty: Easy
Best season: Oct through Mar

Schedule: Open year-round
Traffic: Heavy
Other trail users: Hikers only
Trail surface: Dirt path
Maps: USGS Boquillas

Finding the trailhead: From park headquarters at Panther Junction, drive a little more than 17 miles along the Rio Grande Village highway to the marked Hot Springs turnoff on the right. Follow the maintained dirt road 1.7 miles to the parking lot at its end. The last 0.5 mile or so of the road is very narrow and winding and is impassable to RVs, trailers, or very wide vehicles. Drivers of such vehicles will need to park in a parking area on the right side of the road before the narrow, one-way section of road begins. GPS: N29 10.647' / W102 59.970'

The Hike

J. O. Langford and his family homesteaded here at the confluence of Tornillo Creek and the Rio Grande in 1909 and built a small health spa using hot spring waters. He also hoped to regain his health after suffering from malaria growing up in Mississippi. With the help of a stonemason, he built a large stone bathhouse over the main hot spring. In 1913 unrest and civil war in Mexico caused the Langfords to leave the border area. In 1927 they returned and built a combined post office, trading post, and motel for guests. The Langfords finally left permanently in 1942 after selling their land to the government for inclusion in the new national park. Maggy Smith operated the resort for several more years as a park concession before it finally closed for good.

The ruins of the Livingston house adjoin the trailhead parking lot. Within a few yards the trail passes the relatively intact post office, shaded by a nonnative palm. A short distance beyond the post office on the trail lie the former motel units, with murals painted on the interior walls. A clump of more exotic palms shades the sandy riverbank above the confluence of Tornillo Creek and the river.

Be sure to look closely for painted pictographs on the cliff walls just past the motel units. Various Indian groups lived in and traveled through the area long before the Langfords and other settlers arrived. The trail passes through a short, shady thicket of mesquite, reeds, and other plants before it opens out onto a ledge above the river. The trail follows rock ledges between cliffs above and the river below a short distance to the foundation of the old bathhouse.

The springs gush out 105°F water, filling the foundation and creating a popular natural hot tub. The waters still attract bathers many years after Langford first established the resort. On occasion, when the Rio Grande is high, river waters cover the spring, making bathing impossible. Because of strong currents and hazards made invisible by murky water, the park discourages swimming in the river. In some areas of the West, organisms that live in hot spring water have caused serious health problems when they enter the body through nasal tissues. To avoid any risk, however slight, avoid getting the water into nasal passages.

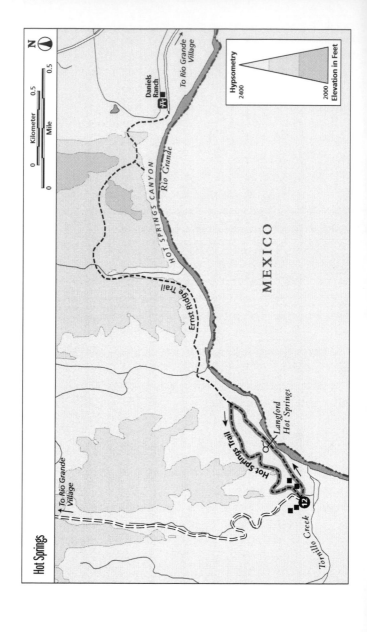

Hot Springs

To Rio Grande Village

Daniels Ranch

HOT SPRINGS CANYON

Rio Grande

Ernst Ridge Trail

To Rio Grande Village

Hot Springs Trail

Langford Hot Springs

Tornillo Creek

MEXICO

12

N

0   0.5   Kilometer
0   0.5   Mile

Hypsometry

2400

2000

Elevation in Feet

Continue the hike by following the trail along the riverbank past the hot spring for about 0.25 mile to a marked junction with the Ernst Ridge Trail. Turn left and climb up onto the bluff above the spring. The route contours along the bluff along an old road before dropping back down to the trailhead parking lot from behind the post office. Because of the climb, the return part of the loop is more difficult, but hikers are well rewarded with broad views of the river, mountains, and desert far south in Mexico.

If time and energy allow, take the Ernst Ridge Trail from its junction with the Hot Springs Trail about 2.5 miles east to Rio Grande Village. It offers tremendous views like the upper part of the Hot Springs Trail loop. However, this trail is considerably more difficult than the Hot Springs Trail, so be sure you are fit, carrying plenty of water, and have cool weather before taking it.

Miles and Directions

0.0   Start at the Hot Springs parking lot. Bear right on the Hot Springs Trail.

0.1   Pass old motel units and pictographs.

0.25 Reach the hot spring.

0.5   Junction with the Ernst Ridge Trail. Bear left, up the hill.

1.0   Arrive back at the Hot Springs parking lot.

13 Rio Grande Village Nature Trail

A day hike from the Rio Grande Village Campground to the Nature Trail Overlook and back.

Elevation range: 1,820–1,960 feet

Distance: 0.75-mile loop

Hiking time: About 30 minutes

Difficulty: Easy

Best season: Oct through Mar

Schedule: Open year-round

Traffic: Heavy

Other trail users: Hikers only

Trail surface: Boardwalk and dirt path

Maps: USGS Boquillas

Finding the trailhead: The trailhead is located across the road from campsite 18 in the Rio Grande Village Class A Campground. Parking is limited at the trailhead; park instead near the registration sign for the campground and walk to site 18. GPS: N29 10.744' / W102 57.244'

The Hike

The Rio Grande Village Nature Trail is an easy walk that takes the hiker through very diverse ecosystems and shows the different human lifestyles practiced on opposite sides of the Rio Grande. The trail begins with a 150-foot boardwalk that crosses a wetland created by a beaver dam and fed by a warm spring. The abundant springwater allows for plants and animals not normally associated with desert settings. Willows, reeds, insects, and fish make their home in this special ecosystem. The uncommon habitat is also a haven for many species of birds.

As you climb the hill leaving the spring area, note the dramatic change in the surrounding environment. Not only does the plant life make an abrupt change, turning to desert scrub and cacti, but even the air becomes drier. At the top of the hill, the loop trail forks. Take the trail to the right.

At the next trail junction, only a short distance down the path, you can see the tiny village of Ojo Caliente, Spanish for "hot spring," across the Rio Grande. This village is an ejido, a Mexican communal landholding where the agricultural products of the land are owned individually by ejido members, although they own the land jointly. A natural hot spring provides water for irrigation at this settlement and makes farming possible. Like the warm spring near the boardwalk, the presence of water at Ojo Caliente creates a moist environment in the desert, allowing the villagers to grow crops sufficient to support themselves and to perhaps trade or sell to nearby settlements.

Take the optional short spur trail to the right, and walk toward the edge of the Rio Grande. Along the trail, watch for rocks containing the fossils of marine creatures, evidence that this area was once covered by an ancient sea. Farther along you'll see other signs of past life in the rocks—round, deep mortar holes that were used by prehistoric people to grind seeds, roots, and pods. Just a short distance farther, you'll encounter the Rio Grande, a ribbon of life through the heart of the dry Chihuahuan Desert.

After exploring the riverbank, return to the spur trail junction and continue along the loop to the right. The impressive limestone cliffs rising high above and across the river are part of the mountain range known as the Sierra del Carmen. Located in Mexico, the towering, banded cliffs are visible from many parts of Big Bend National Park.

As you hike up and around the hill, the village of Boquillas del Carmen comes into view. This remote village near the mouth of Boquillas Canyon has only a small number of residents. In the early 1900s Boquillas was a booming mining town of about 1,000 people who worked nearby lead, zinc, silver, and fluorite mines. Today, subsistence agriculture and tourism support the residents of Boquillas. Because of border restrictions after the tragedy of September 11, 2001, it was not legal to cross over the river to Boquillas for more than ten years. However, it is again possible to cross if you have a passport by going to the Port of Entry along the nearby road to Boquillas Canyon. Be sure to check for the Port of Entry's operating schedule at a park visitor center or online before making the drive. The schedule varies depending on the time of year and the day of the week.

At the next trail junction, turn left and walk to the top of the hill on another short spur trail. From this high vantage point, enjoy the magnificent panorama spread before you. It includes the Rio Grande, the Chisos Mountains, Rio Grande Village, the Sierra del Carmen, two Mexican settlements, and vast expanses of Mexico. The difference in lifestyle on opposite sides of the river is evident; the Rio Grande Village Campground with its modern conveniences contrasts with the rural subsistence lifestyle of Ojo Caliente and Boquillas, Mexico. Also evident is the contrast of the lush vegetation of the warm springs and river with the arid Chihuahuan Desert. The variety of ecosystems and lifestyles along the Rio Grande is what gives the area much of its charm and richness. Now retrace your steps back off the hilltop to the trail junction and turn left. Walk downhill to the next trail junction, the start of the loop, and turn right to return to the campground trailhead.

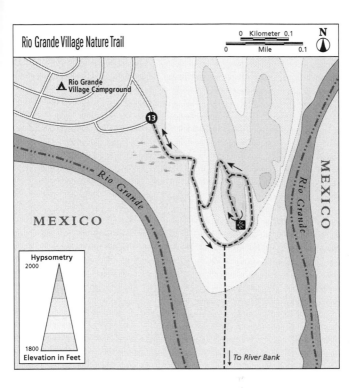

Miles and Directions

0.0 Start at the trailhead in Rio Grande Village Campground.

0.1 Loop begins at the trail junction. Bear right.

0.2 Spur trail to the river goes off to the right.

0.4 Spur trail to hilltop goes off to left.

0.65 The loop ends. Go right.

0.75 Arrive back at the trailhead.

14 Boquillas Canyon

A day hike into the entrance of Boquillas Canyon, one of three major canyons in Big Bend National Park carved by the Rio Grande.

Elevation range: 1,800–1,890 feet
Distance: 0.7 mile one way
Hiking time: About 30 minutes one way
Difficulty: Easy
Best season: Oct through Mar
Schedule: Open year-round

Traffic: Heavy
Other trail users: Hikers only
Trail surface: Dirt path
Maps: USGS Boquillas
Special considerations: Vehicle break-ins are occasionally a problem here; do not leave valuables in your car.

Finding the trailhead: From park headquarters at Panther Junction, drive about 20 miles southeast toward Rio Grande Village. Turn left onto the Boquillas Canyon road just before entering Rio Grande Village and drive 4 miles to the parking lot at the end of the road, where the trail begins. GPS: N29 12.053' / W102 55.172'

The Hike

Boquillas means "little mouths" in Spanish. Although no one is sure where the name for the canyon originated, some believe it was named either for the canyon's narrow entrance or for the numerous small openings, or solution holes, in its limestone walls. The Boquillas Canyon Trail is a popular short trail, appropriate for adults and children. Be aware, however, that during late spring, summer, and early fall, mid-day temperatures frequently rise above 100°F. During the hot time of year, walks along this trail are best taken in the early-morning hours.

From the parking area, the trail immediately climbs about 50 feet onto a low ridge then levels off as the Rio Grande comes into view. The route is lined with typical Chihuahuan Desert vegetation such as creosote bush, lechuguilla, leatherstem, ocotillo, and several varieties of prickly pear cactus. A few yards farther on, the trail splits. If you go to the right, you will skirt a small hill and descend toward the river. Choose the left-hand path to climb up a slight rise and discover an excellent view of the Rio Grande and the entrance to Boquillas Canyon. Looking west from here, you can see the village of Boquillas, Mexico, across the river. About 175 people inhabit the former mining town.

The short left-hand trail rejoins the main trail a bit down the hill via a series of steep log steps. The trail takes you down about 90 feet to the banks of the Rio Grande. Upon reaching the river level, the main trail turns to the left (east). Walk right (west) for about 50 feet, however, and you find yourself on a rock ledge in which there are several mortar holes made by prehistoric people who once lived in this area. Mortar holes like these, used for grinding seeds, roots, and pods, can be found throughout Big Bend. Although the exact age of the mortar holes is unknown, their presence near desert springs and the river underscores the importance of reliable water sources to former inhabitants.

Returning to the main trail, you parallel the river and wind through tunnels of river cane, primarily non-native giant reed. Some of the smaller, native common reed is mixed in; distinguish the two by looking for the erect seed heads of the non-native and the drooping seed heads of the

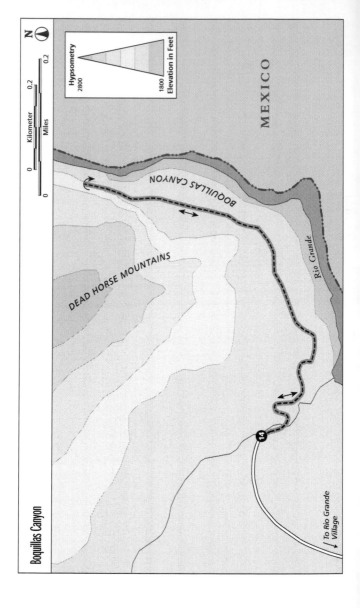

Boquillas Canyon

Hypsometry

2800

1800

Elevation in Feet

Kilometer

Miles

0.2

0.2

N

DEAD HORSE MOUNTAINS

BOQUILLAS CANYON

Rio Grande

MEXICO

14

To Rio Grande
Village

native cane. This section of trail can be washed out or impassable at times due to river flooding, especially in late summer and early fall. Here and everywhere along the river, be careful if you walk along the banks. The river's surface hides deep holes and strong undercurrents.

The trail opens up to a large rocky beach at the edge of the Rio Grande in the entrance to this magnificent limestone canyon. Directly ahead, you can see a fault line in the limestone cliff on the Mexican side of the river; it is obvious where the left-hand side of the fault dropped in relation to the right side. Downstream of the rocky beach, further travel stops where the river cuts off the beach and flows against the canyon wall. To return to the parking lot, retrace your steps.

Miles and Directions

0.0 Start at the Boquillas Canyon trailhead.

0.7 Reach the end of the trail where the Rio Grande cuts off the riverbank.

15 Dog Canyon

A day hike across desert flats on the north side of the park to Dog Canyon, a deep cut through the Dead Horse Mountains.

Elevation range: 2,580–2,520 feet

Distance: 2.5 miles one way

Hiking time: 1.5–2 hours one way

Difficulty: Easy to moderate; does require some modest route-finding

Best season: Oct through Mar

Schedule: Open year-round

Traffic: Light

Other trail users: Equestrians possible but not likely

Trail surface: Dirt path, cobbles, sand, and gravel of a desert wash

Maps: USGS Bone Spring, Dagger Flat

Finding the trailhead: The hike begins at the Dog Canyon Exhibit at a roadside pullout on the east side of the road about 3.5 miles south of the Persimmon Gap Visitor Center (or about 24 miles north of Panther Junction on the road to Marathon). The pullout is about 0.25 mile north of the bridge over Bone Spring Draw. GPS: N29 37.315' / W103 08.571'

The Hike

This route can be traveled any season of the year. However, if you are hiking between mid-April and the end of September, this can be a very hot walk. There is no shade until you get to Dog Canyon and no water. During the hot time of year, plan this walk during early-morning hours.

This well-worn route is easy to follow because the destination, Dog Canyon, is easily visible for the entire hike. From the roadside pullout, Dog Canyon appears as a vertical gash slicing through the mountains about 2.5 miles east. To the north of Dog Canyon, the mountains are called the Santiago Mountains; to the south, the Dead Horse Mountains. Both are part of a long chain of mountains stretching from near Alpine, Texas, deep into Mexico. In Mexico the range is called the Sierra del Carmen.

From the parking lot, the obvious path leads east across the desert flats. If you stray from the trail, just follow your eyes; as stated before, Dog Canyon is always in sight.

The limestone Santiago and Dead Horse Mountains roughly mark the eastern boundary of Big Bend National Park. Limestones of the Santa Elena Formation form the cliff faces along the ridgetops; other geologic layers, prone to faster erosion, lie below. As these lower layers of rock weather away, the massive upper layers of Santa Elena Limestone are undercut and eventually collapse. A prominent scar, visible just north of Dog Canyon, formed from a thundering landslide in 1987. To highlight how distances can be deceiving in the desert, guess how large the boulders are within the debris pile. One of the huge rocks would fill your average-size kitchen.

About 0.25 mile into the hike, look for what appears to be a sidewalk to nowhere running north–south across the path. The pavement is what remains of an early road built decades ago. Also in this area are some small hills to the north and south that seem to contain concentric rings outlining their contours. Thin beds of Boquillas Limestone make up these hills and give them their appearance.

A field guide to Texas grasses is particularly valuable on this hike. At least a dozen species maintain a tenuous foothold in this stretch of desert flats. Although sparse, the diversity of grass species enduring in this hot, dry environment seems remarkable. However, if you study reports from early explorers or diaries from the first homesteaders, you read of an environment far different from what we see today. Their descriptions report a "sea of grass" in much of what today are mostly desert scrublands or bare patches of soil. Through overgrazing and decades of drought, the grasses disappeared. As the grasses were grazed off, fragile desert topsoil eroded away during heavy rains, and desert shrubs invaded. The land lost its water-holding capability, and water tables fell. Fire prevention and changes in rodent populations exacerbated the situation. In only a few decades, mankind greatly changed the land at Big Bend. Even with creation of the park nearly eighty years ago, the land has only partly recovered.

Typical of the Chihuahuan Desert, cacti abound on these flats. A hike during late winter or spring would be the best time to catch prickly pear, pitaya, tasajillo, and dog cactus in bloom. Traveling in February, you might locate a mariposa cactus, one of the earliest cacti to flower, in full bloom. Later in the season, after any rainstorm, look for the beautiful pink flowers of eagle claw cacti. About two-thirds of the way to Dog Canyon, you will pass a population of Torrey's yucca. Like most of the other plant species along this route, the yuccas bloom around March.

Except during early morning or evening, you probably will not see any animals. However, if you look carefully, their signs are all around. Listen for sparrows and thrashers rustling in the desert scrub and the call of the cactus wren. Mammals use the trail, so keep an eye open for javelina and mule deer tracks. There are many burrows and holes tunneled into the desert floor that belong to creatures like badgers, ground squirrels, and tarantulas. The call of a coyote is commonplace throughout this uninhabited corner of the park, particularly early or late in the day. Animal scat litters the terrain, obvious signs that wildlife does indeed survive in this harsh area.

About 0.5 mile from the canyon, the route drops down into Nine Point Draw. Dry most of the year, the arroyo can carry a raging flood after a thunderstorm. Nine Point Draw and its tributaries, such as Bone Spring Draw, provide drainage for much of this part of the park and can easily fill bank to bank with a dangerous, muddy torrent.

Follow the arroyo downstream and it will take you directly into Dog Canyon. Note the vegetation paralleling the walls of Nine Point Draw. Although you will probably not encounter any surface water, precious reserves of moisture usually do exist within desert arroyos. Near these drainages, water becomes trapped from rainstorms and stored under the surface. Even though the amounts are sometimes small, the water reserves are nonetheless enough to create significant changes in the desert habitat. Note how this particular drainage is thickly lined with desert willow, Texas persimmon, Mexican buckeye, and other shrubs and small trees that could never survive in the more arid areas only 100 feet away from the arroyo.

As you enter Dog Canyon, the arroyo walls quickly gain height and change from gravel alluvium to massive limestone layers. In places the gorge contains small caves that give the appearance of limestone dissolving away. In other areas the old grayish rock surface has eroded off, uncovering a fresh interior that contributes an orange color to the cliff faces.

The geologic highlight of Dog Canyon is its south wall, just before you exit the far end. There the once-horizontal layers of rock have been uplifted and now lie in a slightly curved vertical formation. Erosion has chiseled away some of the layers faster than others, creating an unusual appearance.

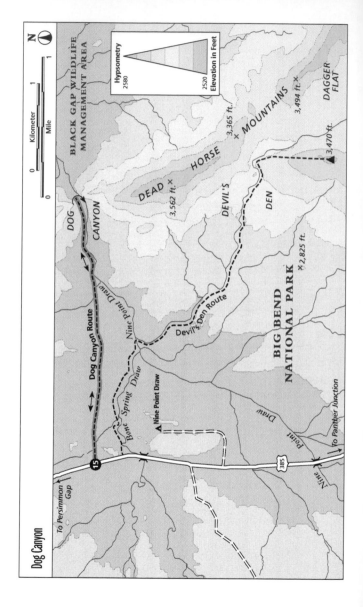

Dog Canyon

To hike back, retrace your steps, but watch for where the trail leaves Nine Point Draw on the north side and heads back across the desert flats. If you miss the spot, you can follow the drainage back to the road, but it will add some distance to the hike. If you do follow the draw back to the highway, be sure to turn right at the road and follow it back north to the trailhead. Before you depart for the return trek, however, take a moment to relax in the cool confines of this short canyon.

The nearby Devil's Den hike is very worthwhile, too. It's relatively easy, but it's a more primitive route that requires strong hiker experience, a good hike description such as found in *Hiking Big Bend National Park*, a good map, and a GPS and/or compass to complete.

Miles and Directions

0.0 Start at the trailhead at Dog Canyon Exhibit.

2.5 Arrive at Dog Canyon.

Suggested Reading

Clark, Gary, and Kathy Adams Clark. *Enjoying Big Bend National Park*. College Station, TX: Texas A&M University Press, 2009.

Parent, Laurence, and Joe Nick Patoski. *Big Bend National Park*. Austin, TX: University of Texas Press, 2006.

Parent, Laurence. *Death in Big Bend*. Houston, TX: Iron Mountain Press, 2010.

Parent, Laurence. *Scenic Driving Texas*. Essex, CT: Globe Pequot, 2023.

Parent, Laurence. *Hiking Big Bend National Park*. Essex, CT: FalconGuides, 2022.

About the Author

Laurence Parent was born in New Mexico and raised there and in Arizona. After receiving an engineering degree at the University of Texas at Austin, he practiced engineering for six years before becoming a full-time freelance photographer and writer specializing in landscape, travel, and nature subjects. His photos appear in Sierra Club, Audubon, Brown-Trout, and many other calendars. Article and photo credits include *National Geographic Traveler*, *Outside*, *Backpacker*, *Sierra*, and the *New York Times*. He contributes regularly to regional publications such as *Texas Highways*, *Texas Monthly*, *Arizona Highways*, *New Mexico Magazine*, and *Texas Parks & Wildlife*. Other work includes commercial assignments, architectural photography, ranch photography, advertising, museum exhibits, postcards, and brochures.

Parent has completed more than forty-five books, including seven other guidebooks for FalconGuides / Globe Pequot: *Hiking New Mexico*, *Hiking Texas*, *Scenic Driving New Mexico*, *Scenic Driving Wyoming*, *Scenic Driving North Carolina*, *Hiking Big Bend National Park*, and *Scenic Driving Texas*. One of his latest works is *Texas: Portrait of a State*, a large-format coffee-table book produced by Graphic Arts Books. Although he lived in Texas for many years, he now makes his home in Prescott, Arizona, with his wife, Patricia, and their two children.

THE TEN ESSENTIALS OF HIKING

American Hiking Society

Whether you plan to be gone for a couple of hours or several months, make sure to pack these items. Become familiar with these items and know how to use them.

Find other helpful resources at AmericanHiking.org/hiking-resources.

 1. Appropriate Footwear

 2. Navigation

 3. Water (and a way to purify it)

 4. Food

 5. Rain Gear & Dry-Fast Layers

 6. Safety Items (light, fire, and a whistle)

 7. First Aid Kit

 8. Knife or Multi-Tool

 9. Sun Protection

 10. Shelter

PROTECT THE PLACES YOU LOVE TO HIKE

Become a member today and take $5 off an annual membership using the code **Falcon5**.

AmericanHiking.org/join

American Hiking Society is the only national nonprofit organization dedicated to empowering all to enjoy, share, and preserve the hiking experience.